THE IMAGE
OF LEADERSHIP

THE IMAGE
OF LEADERSHIP

How leaders package themselves
to stand out for the right reasons

BY

SYLVIE DI GIUSTO

Executive Image Consulting

ISBN: 978-0-9904088-8-8 (Hardcover)
ISBN: 978-0-9904088-3-3 (Paperback)
Also available as an e-Book

People Packaging
Is What I Do...

Contents

About the Author

With more than twenty years of corporate experience educating and inspiring thousands of clients across Europe and around the world, Sylvie di Giusto, Personal Branding Strategist and Image Expert, empowers people to influence the success of their own careers. Her passion for fashion inspired her to launch Executive Image Consulting, based in New York City. It is here that she uses her extensive corporate expertise to help her valued clients project a powerful visual image of themselves to the outside world.

Throughout her career, Sylvie has held senior positions, primarily within human resources, for organizations ranging in size from ten to one hundred thousand employees, including BMW, BASF, Bayer, Henkel, McKinsey, and Thomas Cook. She's become a recognized member of the international business community because she has worked with every strata of management from CEOs to young executives within the finance, automotive, pharmaceutical, food, retail, consulting, entertainment and tourism industries. As a speaker retained by companies, an effective trainer, an experienced coach, and an enthusiastic workshop leader, Sylvie knows the challenges faced by professionals in their workplace. Using a results-orientated approach, she has a proven track record in corporate and individual counseling.

Living abroad has enabled Sylvie to gain further qualifications in her field from the Fashion Institute of Technology in New York, and from the Academy of Professional Image and the International Academy of Image and Style in Australia. She is an active member of the Association for International Image Consultants, the National Association of Professional Women and the National Speakers Association.

Austrian by birth, French in her heart, Italian in her kitchen, German in her work ethic, and American by choice, Sylvie has lived a varied life traveling the world and accomplishing personal and professional goals. Her life is rich with unique experiences, not to mention the joy of raising her two wonderful children in New York City with her husband. When she's not working, Sylvie volunteers her time with New York Cares; when she's not volunteering, she enjoys spending time with her family both exploring New York City and traveling throughout the United States—the amazing city and country she feels lucky to call home.

About "Tweet This"

In this book I've included tweetable statements to each chapter. My thoughts and comments round off every chapter with a short and sweet tweet. People I adore and value for their point of view introduce each chapter to you with a tweet. I've also reached out to the amazing group of followers, fans and colleagues I'm surrounded by, and many of them made their opinion heard by tweeting about #TheImageOfLeadership.

It's our chance to meet each other—you and me, my followers and all the readers of this book. Just tweet the suggested statement, choose one or two, or each. It doesn't matter, as long as you tweet it to start the conversation with each other. I encourage you to reach out to the amazing group of people who provided tweets for this book. I handpicked each of them, and I'm proud and thankful for their contributions.

I invite you to also tweet about anything you find in this book or any thoughts you might have related to this book. Just make sure you hashtag your tweets with
#TheImageOfLeadership.

I'll find you! I promise.
Happy tweeting!

Foreword
by Jeffrey W. Hayzlett

My idea of marketing is to focus on products and services from the inception of an idea all the way through to customer satisfaction. Marketing is a combination of critical thinking, strategy, and analytics, facts and gut instinct. It's much more than communications or advertising. Those days are dead. Where many thought the CMO was really the Chief Advertising Officer, where advertising was more aligned as being marketing, is over. Done. For me, marketing is thorough, thought provoking, challenging, and about delivery on the promise of the brand.

Sylvie di Giusto presents my idea of marketing in her new and exciting have-to-have book: *The Image of Leadership:* How leaders package themselves to stand out for the right reasons.

I have always said a brand is a promise declared. Sylvie demonstrates how it's up to you:

- you are the product and the service
- you need to look at yourself from inception to customer satisfaction
- you need to learn how to leave a positive professional—and personal—imprint
- you need to know all of the steps to market yourself

Sylvie says, "People packaging is what I do." She is right. And she is great at it.

I often talk about how we have to change our attitude to change our business and change our future. In *The Image of Leadership*, Sylvie applies the need for change to your personal and professional imprint. It is difficult to be a leader if you are not leaving a positive imprint. Change is often necessary if you expect to have a positive imprint and have the "look of leadership."

Yet, just like in business, we get stuck in our old ways of doing things. We know people resist change, especially when it comes to their personal style! I shout from the rooftops: "Change has never killed anybody." Sylvie shows us how to change and leave a positive imprint.

In my book, *The Mirror Test* I describe how you need to be pitch perfect in your presentations. I found that the length of time the average person may concentrate on something and not lose focus is 8 seconds—so those first 8 seconds are the key. I believe you have 8 seconds to hook someone and you have another 110 seconds to reel them in.

If I am engaged, I will lean in during those first 8 seconds and then there are another 110 seconds for me to buy the idea. Less than 2 minutes… thumbs up or thumbs down…that fast.

Sylvie is saying to forget the 110 seconds. Forget the 8 seconds. Her research and experience shows we only have 7 seconds to leave an impression—be it a great impression or a lousy impression. 7 seconds!

You may have a great idea which is the next Google or Facebook. And, if in those first 7 seconds you don't provide an appealing professional imprint to your listener—it doesn't matter what you say. You may talk for the 110 seconds. You may talk for 30 minutes. But you won't get the results you want because they won't really be listening. They dismissed you in their mind in the first 7 seconds.

Those are tough numbers.

In *The Image of Leadership*, Sylvie combines my marketing requirements of critical thinking and gut instinct. She uses scientific research, her years of experience, and, interestingly, her unique view as a European, to hone in on everything you need to do to improve your professional imprint.

Step-by-step, Sylvie walks you through how to market yourself and help you get to where you want to go. Your presence, your style, your approach, your communications skills…everything is considered.

She uses an ABCD approach for you to always have the positive professional imprint you need:

- Appearance: She helps you analyze every visual element of yourself, which is seen and understood by others in those first 7 seconds.

- Behavior: She has you take a critical look at your attitude—the sum of your actions—which demonstrate leadership.

- Communication: She has you review your communication skills. Do you communicating concisely? Effectively? Clearly? Do you demonstrate continuity and reliability so people trust what you are saying?

- Digital Footprint: How do you present yourself on the internet? This is becoming increasingly crucial with the prevalence of social media.

Sylvie does not advocate a "one-size-fits-all" formula in *The Image of Leadership*. People have different styles and different career aspirations. They come from different industries and hold different positions. She urges you to both accept who you are and to make the most of who you are. It seems contrarian—yet her approach works.

She gives you great ideas and talks about body shapes, height, and weight. She discusses how age and gender impact your look. She has you focus on authenticity in your personal presentation.

Sylvie is thoughtful in her approach and, at the same time, she does not pull any punches. She gives you valuable insight drawn from her many years of experience. She makes the read worth your while.

Sylvie's bottom line is there is "no excuse for unprofessional appearance." This is something all of us need to hear—no excuse. We have no excuse not to make the best of our being, our resources, and our outlook so we always look our best in every professional setting. Every time! No excuses!

The Image of Leadership is a great book, which gives you a thorough, thought provoking, and challenging way to market yourself. So remember:

…You have 7 seconds…

…You won't have many first chances…you'll get even fewer second chances…and you'll never have any third chances…

…You have to be ready every time…

…And Sylvie di Giusto will always have you ready for those critical 7 seconds with *The Image of Leadership*.

Jeffrey W. Hayzlett
Primetime TV Show Host, Bestselling Author & Sometime Cowboy

Preface

I have a wonderful job. I work with bright, enthusiastic people who either want to advance their careers or simply want to feel more confident about themselves. I believe that when you look good you feel good, and that people around you feel your confidence and respond positively. I've learned this from experience. Having served in executive positions related to human resources for over twenty years, I've had the opportunity to both observe and influence many career paths. And, to be very honest, it often frustrated me to see how many unqualified poseurs are given positions of great responsibility in companies. One of the obvious reasons is that these imposters know how to present and sell themselves. Many of them get hired or promoted, only to quickly fail to deliver the performance they promise.

On the other hand, my work with the top talents and high potentials of leading retail and tourism companies has made me aware of the many young, aspiring, talented, hard working and ambitious people who never get the chance because they don't know how to present themselves. Because they don't outwardly resemble the leaders that top employers are seeking, too many doors are closed to them.

There's a very common saying that I'm sure you've heard: "Dress for the job you want to have, not for the one you currently have." I tend not to use this little homily because it sounds so small, so irrelevant, so superficial, and so sketchy. I want my clients to simply focus on their willingness to become *leaders*. And if you want to become a leader, you should look like one long before you are one.

But what defines the look of leadership? I've always been fascinated by leaders who enter a room and everyone stops and notices. They just "appear." And I've wondered what it is that they have and what they all have in common. Do they all look authentic? Professional? Maybe expensive? In my corporate seminars I talk about two examples.

I once worked for a big European retail company that was not doing well due to a challenging market environment. We were also behind the times and did little to modernize our business practices. Our headquarters had the ambiance of an old-fashioned, obviously not up-to-date, struggling company. This was embodied in the appearance of our management team. We all reflected exactly the company's situation.

What we needed was someone new to lead the company: someone modern, open-minded, innovative, and with international experience. Someone with vision. Thankfully, the new CEO who was to lead us through this crisis was exactly whom we were looking for. When he entered the stage to speak to the crowd of leading managers, he "wowed" them from their seats. He appeared on the stage as a slim, tall figure in a well-cut suit, perfect fitted shirt, shiny shoes, elegant tie, and not one hair on his head out of place. Sometimes he just stood there, saying nothing, and the crowd applauded him just for being there, representing us and our company in our dark, old-fashioned, musty headquarters.

One of his first strategic decisions was to merge our company with an international tourism company. It was exactly what we were hoping for! We joined forces with a world leader and we became international. At our yearly management conference we met their CEO. He was one of the most inspiring leaders I've ever seen, and yet his style was completely different from the CEO of our company. He was, I suppose, exactly what you'd expect from the leader of a tourism company. He looked like he just came from a two-week vacation—deeply tanned, and with circles under his eyes that suggested long nights in some exotic Caribbean bar. When he entered the stage everybody thought for a moment: "Huh? Who's that?" He wore some kind of nondescript suit, no tie, with his shirt collar unbuttoned, and somehow his entire leadership crew looked like that. They all looked like they just came from vacation. Guess what? Their business was obviously vacations, and it totally worked. He opened his mouth and he instantly had us all. He made jokes that no one else could have made on stage, and he received several standing ovations. He was in total control of the audience.

Two executives—both of them very convincing, with two different signature styles. Both were charismatic leaders who captivated their audiences and left their employees with a powerful first impression. While in the long run they both faced very difficult business challenges

The Image of Leadership by Sylvie di Giusto

and eventually left the company, the important thing is that they got our attention and the door to leadership was opened for them.

Over the years I've learned that while there are things that you absolutely need to know about how to present yourself in public and on the job, there is no one-size-fits-all formula. You are unique. Your situation and your aspirations are unique.

Whether you're running for public office, seeking a plum promotion, making a big sales call, or having dinner with someone special, I want those around you to have confidence in you. I hope this book helps you to become your best possible authentic self, so that people see you as a leader and so that you see yourself as a leader. It's all about bringing the interior and exterior into alignment, and realizing your highest personal potential.

Sylvie di Giusto @Sylvie_diGiusto
"There is no one-size-fits-all formula. You are unique.
Your situation and your aspirations are unique."
#TheImageOfLeadership

Introduction

Welcome to *The Image of Leadership*. The title reflects the reality that everyone can and should acknowledge, which is that true leadership manifests itself in ways that are both seen and unseen. They are equally important. While all leaders have their own individual styles and personalities, it cannot be doubted that the most effective leaders who succeed over a long period of time are seen and accepted because their interior skills and exterior images are in perfect alignment. In other words, what you see is what you get. As leaders they are consistent and dependable, and their professional imprint—which I'll introduce to you and talk about in the book—is strong and durable.

On your personal journey towards leadership—whether it's in the workplace, in politics, or in your community—something that I truly believe in is this: you must *look like* a leader long before you *are one*.

If you're already in a position of leadership, you might think, is this book for me? Is it only for beginners? My answer is that this book is definitely for you. If you think it through to its conclusion, you'll find that what I say is true throughout every strata of management and leadership responsibility. There is always the next step up. You have to look like someone who is prepared for a C-level position long before you are in the circle of C-level executives. You have to be identifiable as a possible candidate for a board of director's seat long before you are one. You have to look like the president of the United States before you become the president. (There are plenty of senators, representatives, and state governors who do not yet look presidential.) Therefore, the main setting and significance of this statement is always the same, no matter if you're at the beginning of your career or at a very high level. I have often thought whether there are other factors that may be more relevant the higher you are on the career ladder, such as your network, office politics, or cronyism; however, I see no difference between the drama in a small department and that in the boardroom.

This book will take you step by step through the development of your professional imprint. The focus will be on all of those things that people perceive about you, with an emphasis on your appearance and your image. I mean your image as you sit behind your desk, address a group of colleagues, appear on television, or go to a job interview. It's based on the proven concept that you cannot simply *tell* people that you're a leader and expect them to treat you as one. You have to *show* people your leadership, every day, consistently, and in a way that encourages them to voluntarily accept you as being someone in whom they will place their trust.

We'll begin with the seven-second rule. This is that brief moment in time when others first see you, whether it's at a meeting, on the job, or at an interview. They may have some prior knowledge of you, but this is the first time they actually lay eyes on you. I'll show you how people make up their minds very quickly about your leadership potential, and either open the door for you or slam it shut. The good thing is that this process is entirely under your control. You can choose to present yourself as a leader, or not.

I'll reveal the components of your professional imprint, and how, after it's been established in those first seven seconds, you need to sustain it over time. I'll show you the ABCDs of your professional imprint—appearance, behavior, communication, and digital footprint, which in our wired culture is becoming increasingly important.

While how you dress is very important, this is not a how-to book. I'm not going to detail specific items of clothing or accessories that you need to buy or wear. What I want to provide for you is a deep understanding of the concepts that you need to put into practice in your own way. I want to give you the power to create your own professional imprint that is true to your personality and that works for you for the duration of your long career.

I'll talk about what's under your clothes—your body, and how your confidence in yourself can transcend any physical shortcomings that you think you might have. You can be any height, weight, color, or gender, and be perceived as a leader. How? By being authentic. By not being phony, and by being on the inside what people perceive on the outside.

We all understand that leaders appear in various contexts, from the boardroom to the tennis court. To give you some specific guidance, I'll reveal the +1/-1 rule, which sets up a scale of dressing from casual to professional. As you'll see, it's all a matter of knowing what to wear that's appropriate for the occasion. Leaders don't wear business suits on the tennis court; they wear perfectly coordinated and fitted tennis clothing.

Is this book going to stifle your personality? Absolutely not. The goal of this book is to remove unhelpful distractions that prevent people from seeing the leadership that you can offer. It offers freedom from bad choices that hinder communication. And besides, what's more valuable to you: your right to wear jeans to work, or the opportunity to rise to an executive position and make a real difference to your company and your community?

You'll find some tough talk in this book about touchy topics like body odor and personal grooming. But it's better that you hear it from me, your friendly image consultant, than you hear it from your boss or, worse, read about it on a snarky social media page.

In this book I'm going to discuss politicians and people in the public eye. My choices have nothing to do with my own political beliefs, nor am I interested in the political decisions or business decisions those people have made or will made. Instead, as an image consultant I've learned to step back and look at any person from a very neutral position. It's convenient for us to discuss people who are in the public eye, and I can assume you know them and can easily find images of them online. Which proves my point: if you're in a position of leadership and you wear a bizarre dress or have a weird orange suntan or display bad teeth, you can bet that it will be all over the Internet.

Leaders come in all shapes and sizes—including yours! This book can help you develop your professional imprint and become the leader that you deserve to be. It's all a matter of letting people see the star that is ready to shine.

Let's get started on your exciting journey to achieving your full leadership potential.

🐦 Sylvie di Giusto @Sylvie_diGiusto
"You must look like a leader long before you are one."
#TheImageOfLeadership

Chapter 1
Seven Seconds

 Fatima Sheikh @FSCharlie
"Invite people in to see how
incredible you are. Your image
lets people understand you're
worth opening doors for."
#TheImageOfLeadership

Appearances matter. Every hour of every day, we humans evaluate our environment based on what we see and hear. We avoid situations and people that seem threatening. We gravitate towards situations and people that appear welcoming. When we meet someone, we use sensory information to quickly determine if we're going to get along with them or if we need to keep our distance. We turn on the television and say, "This show looks good. I think I'll watch it." At the store, we inspect the food that we want to buy. When a dog approaches on the street, before we extend our hand we look for its body language. Is the tail wagging, or is the dog tense?

Just as we judge others, we are judged by the people who meet us or see us in the media. Do we appear trustworthy? Confident? Or do we appear uncertain or detached? People whom we meet make decisions about us. Should they hire us? Vote for us? Buy something from us?

Anyone who aspires to a position of leadership in any capacity needs to understand the power of image. The good news is that your image is something you can control. You can make it what you want. I'm not talking about how tall or short you are, or what color. I'm talking about the message you send to the people who see you and interact with you. It's a combination of your dress, your attitude, and how you communicate. These are all things that you can shape and mold to work in your favor, and help you to rise to the level of leadership to which you aspire.

🐦 **Brad Kellum @bradkellum**
"You need to take some steps back to see how others see you. Only then can you catch a glimpse of self." #TheImageOfLeadership

Let's start with a story. It's about two people who are applying for an executive position. It represents a tremendous opportunity and both of our friends want to make a good impression. Their names are Charlie and Roger. For the sake of comparison they're both men, but of course they could just as easily both be women. While the story centers around getting hired, the principles revealed in the story are true across any situation: leading a company, running for public office, or standing in front of a group and giving a speech.

First, let's meet Charlie. With high hopes of landing the position, he waits in the lobby of the corporate headquarters. Judy, the human resources manager, enters the lobby and introduces herself. She smiles and shakes his hand before inviting him to her office. As they walk down the short hallway the manager says nothing. When they reach her office, Judy offers Charlie a seat before circling around to her chair behind her desk. After sitting down she gives Charlie a perfunctory smile and reads his résumé. Her questions are polite and businesslike. She asks him about his experience and what he thinks he can bring to the company.

During the interview Charlie has an uneasy feeling. He doesn't think that he's connecting with the manager. He's qualified for the position—his résumé is what got him the interview—but he gets the impression that Judy wants something more from him. He feels the moment slipping away, like water through his fingers. He can't quite define the problem—perhaps, he thinks to himself, she's just a bit of a cold fish. After all, she interviews people all day, so maybe she's just going through the motions and giving him the same treatment she gives everyone else.

After twenty minutes Judy snaps shut Charlie's file folder and says, "Well, then, do you have any questions?"

Charlie has a million questions, but the manager's coolness has him flustered. He replies that he doesn't have any questions before asking what the next step will be.

"As I'm sure you must understand," Judy says, "we have quite a few applicants for this position. This first round of interviews is just the beginning of the process. We'll be in touch next week. I want to thank you for your time and for your interest." She stands up and guides Charlie to the door.

As Charlie walks out of the sleek glass doors of the corporate headquarters building, he feels like he's just gotten the bum's rush. His prospects for a call back, he thinks, are not very good.

Now let's see how Roger fares during the same process. On paper, he has the same qualifications as Charlie. In fact, his résumé is identical to Charlie's. He's the same age and the same physical type.

As she did with Charlie, Judy greets Roger in the lobby of the corporate headquarters. She smiles and shakes his hand before inviting him to her office. As they walk down the short hallway Judy turns to ask him questions. Was he able to find the building easily? Would he like some coffee or a soft drink?

When they reach her office she offers Roger a seat before circling around to her chair behind her desk. After sitting down she gives Roger a broad smile before glancing at his résumé. But it's just a glance, because on paper she knows he's qualified. Judy asks him about his experience and what he thinks he can bring to the company. When he mentions a particular project the company is working on, she leans forward and asks him how he would handle it. Then she asks him if he has a few extra minutes to meet the project manager. Roger says sure, no problem. She phones the project manager, who comes to her office. They talk about the project for a while and Roger shares his experience.

An hour after Roger first arrived, Judy says that she really must excuse herself for another appointment, but is Roger free next week? Roger replies that he's available and thanks her for her time.

As Roger walks out of the sleek glass doors of the corporate headquarters building, he feels like he's hit a home run. He made a solid connection with both the human resources manager and the project manager. And he feels good about the next interview he's got lined up for today—it's across town, with the company's number one competitor.

At the human resources staff meeting the next day, the candidates for the position are reviewed. Charlie's name comes up. "No," says Judy flatly. "He's not our type. He didn't seem confident. I can't see him joining our team." Then Roger's name is offered. "Very strong," says Judy. "I immediately got from him a sense of leadership. He has a dynamic personality. I think that if we hired him, he'd hit the ground running."

Charlie and Roger. Two perfectly nice guys with identical résumés. But one was branded a loser, the other a winner.

The amazing thing is that if you asked Judy what it was about them that set them apart, she might not come right out and say that it was how they dressed. But that's what it was. And she might not say that she had made up her mind about Charlie within seven seconds of seeing him in the lobby of the company. The interview? It was just an obligation. A formality. Charlie never had a chance. As soon as she could, Judy cut the interview short and showed him the door.

Among both human resource professionals and other executives, the physical appearance of a candidate or colleague is something people don't discuss overtly. It's something they tend to play down as superficial and not in their own system of values. There are legal issues too. They just cannot tell you, "We won't hire you because we don't like your look." It's amongst the many things that would get them in trouble if they said so. Recruiters probably won't admit that they already think they "know you" before you walk through their door. Because of the résumé you've send in, they have a certain image of you in their head that comes from their theoretical image of someone who could fill this position. They also think they know you from what they've seen online or in social media.

In addition, people think it's not politically correct to judge people by their appearance and to openly admit it. Even recruiters tend to fall silent when you ask them about the direct influence of appearance on their decisions.

An organization itself may be confused about what it expects. Some of them have strict dress code rules, and face the challenge that people don't follow them; others don't have any dress code rules, and give people a hard time for not knowing what's right or wrong. It's one of the hidden, often unspoken things we usually don't like to talk about in the context with our careers—but we obviously enjoy it in a private context.

Everyone knows the old saying, "You can't judge a book by its cover." The hard reality is that every day, in countless similar situations, we're judged by our covers—that is, our clothing, our accessories, our hair, our hands, our shoes. We can say it's not fair, but it's the law of the jungle. We can urge our fellow citizens to look under the surface, and they do, but it takes time—more time than most people have.

The reality is this: When you think about the phrase "dress for success," don't get it wrong. The incorrect look could significantly diminish your chances of getting the job. Our friend Charlie may have sincerely thought that his casual slacks and rumpled jacket were appropriate for the positions that he had held in the past. But when Judy took one look at him, she said to herself, "This guy doesn't understand what our company stands for. And I don't have time to teach him."

Of course, it's absolutely possible that in another industry or even in another department, Charlie's rumpled look might have worked for him. But not with Judy, and not in this situation.

When dressing for an interview, you need to follow the rules of your specific industry. For example, if you're interviewing in a conservative industry like banking or law, a short skirt or plunging neckline isn't appropriate interview attire. When in doubt, err on the side of caution. Before you go on a job interview, do some research on your potential employer's dress code. You can start by asking business associates in your LinkedIn network, visiting the company website, or asking former employees for advice.

A suit may not always be the best choice for what to wear on a job interview. If you arrive wearing a business suit and tie and all the employees at the social media company are wearing t-shirts and jeans, you'll look out of place, feel uncomfortable, and give off the wrong energy. The same is true in reverse. If you show up wearing jeans and a sweatshirt to a company whose employees wear professional attire, you'll just be confirming that you don't fit into the company.

 AgentsinStyle @RhodaWheeler
"Dress Codes are for making everyone feel comfortable."
#TheImageOfLeadership

As for Roger, the moment Judy saw him—even before they shook hands—she knew he was a contender. His suit, his haircut, his choice of necktie, his flawless shoes—all spoke of a man who saw himself as a leader. But it was not vanity that was the source of Roger's impulse to look like a leader. He was no super-slick wannabe anchorman. In fact, his professional appearance was driven by humility. Of course Roger wanted to appear successful, but on a deeper level he wanted to be instantly accepted into the company culture. He wanted Judy to be able to look beyond his clothing and see that he could contribute. He wanted to make his appearance a non-issue. He wanted his peers to trust him and believe that he could get the job done.

He wanted to look like a leader. Not a pompous windbag, but someone who inspired confidence and trust, and who brought out the very best in others.

🐦 Sylvie di Giusto @Sylvie_diGiusto
"The hard reality is that every day, in countless similar situations we're judged by our covers." #TheImageOfLeadership

The Cost of a Poor Professional Imprint

While it's your job to project a positive professional image and reputation, we all know that no one is infallible. In the end every leader is a human being who can make mistakes. Some of those mistakes can be quietly dismissed, while others show up on the first page of Google. It might be that you drunk too much at the company's Christmas party, you really, really, really found that tweet funny and had a great laugh, or that you just didn't have a good hand when choosing this morning's outfit before meeting the CEO of your company. But if you don't strive to maintain the highest possible professional imprint in everything that you do, the consequences might be painful:

- Lower productivity
- Disrespect (from others)
- Distraction (from your work, your performance)
- Preconceptions that can damage your career
- Missed opportunities
- Financial penalties
- Sexual Harassment
- Bullying

You think this sounds far-fetched? Think again. People have lost jobs or elections over far less. Anthony Weiner, former U.S. representative and unsuccessful candidate for mayor of New York City, became notorious for his affinity for sending inappropriate selfies. Paula Deen was fired from the Food Network after admitting to using racial slur. AOL CEO Tim Armstrong's comment about the million-dollar price tag for saving "distressed babies" went viral. Remember Justine Sacco? Probably you don't remember her name, but you might remember the firestorm on Twitter the former PR executive left after a needless and careless tweet about AIDS in Africa.

Even the always-edgy Madonna had to apologize for an Instagram hashtag that used a form of the "n-word." This is true for those who made a mistake by their own, or simply have to take responsibility for someone within their team or company. Papa John's CEO John Schnatter had to apologize for a racist rant a deliveryman left on a customer's voicemail. Mark Lee, the CEO of luxury department store Barneys, had to do the same for two undercover police officers who stopped two African-American customers after making expensive purchases in their store.

It often takes just one moment (or one simple click) and your image is instantly destroyed. If for any reason you have hurt your professional image and your reputation, the good news is, that every image can be repaired. Luckily, we live in a nation of second chances. I'm European, and from this perspective, I can think of many examples of second chances in American politics and life, such as the remarkable image-repairing process Americans have let Bill Clinton go through. He serves as the perfect example for someone who has reformed and rebuilt his professional image.

But you can only make that mistake once. While I believe that this is a country of second chances, I don't think there is space for third ones. Therefore, the first step in order to repair your professional image is, to make sure it doesn't happen again. There is no "second chance" for a "second chance."

🐦 **Sylvie di Giusto @Sylvie_diGiusto**
"It often takes just one moment (or one simple click) and your image
is instantly destroyed." #TheImageOfLeadership

Chapter 2
Your Professional Imprint

 Heidi Deblaere @hdeblaere
"Making a great first impression
is the best way to enhance
your image and get off on
the right foot with others."
#TheImageOfLeadership

While the seven-second rule applies to many of life's everyday encounters, the focus of this book is not on dating but on your professional career. And I'd like to start our discussion with a clarification about terminology. There are many terms that people use; some call it a professional image, others say professional identity, and yet others relate it to personal branding.

I describe it as the *professional imprint* you leave on someone's memory.

The professional imprint occurs within seven seconds. It's quick and indelible. Some studies suggest it takes three seconds or eleven seconds, and they delineate different characteristics you are judged on. The exact length of time doesn't matter. What matters is that this happens automatically in our brains—no matter whether we are aware of it, no matter if we find it fair or not, and no matter if under our shabby clothes we have the soul of Mother Theresa.

Our professional imprint reflects directly what level of care or time we spent on our own valuable assets. Do we rush through our morning routines at the expense of our hair or makeup, or clothes? These important steps that are taken to ensure our best possible foot forward before we leave home directly benefit the organization for which we work.

The reputation of fellow employees depends on the look of a company, and each and every one of the employees must provide their fellow employees or clients with the best possible outward experience they can obtain. A company knows that their employees are a representation of the company itself, and they want your first impression with clients, co-workers, bosses, and stakeholders to leave them with the best possible perception of you as an individual and an employee.

So, is it all about the right outfit? A good outfit is going to help make a good impression within those initial first seconds that you are at any event, but after that first impression, it is up to you. Remember to be confident and prepare for the event.

🐦 **Andrea Hill @andreahill**
"Everything should reflect a company's brand. Even the dress code." #TheImageOfLeadership

While our story of Charlie and Roger centered around a job interview, the so-called seven-second rule applies in countless everyday situations. When you enter a business meeting, meet an investor, appear on cable television, make a sales pitch, campaign for public office, sit before a jury of your peers, take your love interest out on a date—time after time your audience will gather information about you and respond within seven seconds. And once the response is made, it's next to impossible to reverse it. When Judy saw Charlie and placed him in the "loser" category, there was practically nothing he could have done to change it. He was doomed from the start.

The interaction between Judy and Charlie could have occurred in any context. They could have been on a blind date. Charlie could have been a politician seeking her vote. He could have been a business owner seeking an angel investor. It doesn't matter; within seven seconds, given the way he presented himself, Charlie would be consigned to the category of loser.

In contrast, when Judy saw Roger, it took only a moment for her to place him in the category of winner. From that time on, the game was his to either win or lose. He was a contender and the odds were in his favor. That's what I want for all of my clients, and for you: to be instantly considered a winner, and to have every possible opportunity to prove that you're the leader you know you can be.

How you are dressed not only affects how other people perceive you, but how you view yourself. If you look the part, you'll more easily act the part. You'll have more confidence, gain more respect from co-workers, and make a strong impression with clients, supporters, and bosses. It also has an impact on your productivity. This is not only true for those who work in a corporate environment; I very often talk about this topic with people who are small business owners, or who work at home. While what you wear may not directly influence your productivity, your state of mind does. Plus, you never know if your next deal will come from a person you happen to meet, so it's smart to make sure you always portray the same image that you would to a prospective customer or business partner. Choosing how you dress when you work is one of the countless decisions you need to make for yourself as a leader, whether you're self-employed or heading up a multi-national company. It's important to think about how you're perceived when

🐦 **Fatima Sheikh @fscharlie**

"You never know who is waiting to be impressed by your confidence."

#TheImageOfLeadership

you're out and about. Always consider if you'd be comfortable running into a potential work connection. It's not about being someone you're not. It's about affecting others without saying a word.

When you're working in the comfort of your own home, it's easy and understandable to dress down. However, I often remind those clients that the person whom they see most often is themselves. And there is just no doubt that spending their day in pajamas has an influence on the quality and quantity of their work. Why? Simply because your mindset reflects your dress code. When you're dressed professionally, you reflect the professional in you. When you're dressed too casually, it's the other way around. I'm not saying you have to sit there in your power high heels or in a two-piece suit. But there has to be something in between. Again, the person you see most often each day is yourself. Make sure that you always perceive yourself as the professional leader you want to be.

Society's preoccupation with, and marketing of, physical attractiveness reinforces the assumption that being good-looking pays bigger benefits than it actually does. The undeniable truth is that being attractive can be a huge asset.

Many of these studies are summarized and discussed in the 2011 book *Beauty Pays: Why Attractive People Are More Successful*, written by Daniel Hamermesh, an economist at the University of Texas in Austin. The research reviewed by Hamermesh shows that attractive people earn an average of three or four percent more than people with below average looks. These people are also hired sooner, get promotions more quickly, are higher-ranking in their companies, and get all kinds of extra benefits. Why? It turns out that more attractive people often bring more money to their companies, and are therefore more valuable employees.

I'm not talking about your DNA. It's not about how tall you are or your body type, although this plays a role, as you will find out later in this book. I'm talking about the countless things that you can do—regardless of the qualities bestowed upon you by the vagaries of the genetic lottery—to develop your best qualities (we all have them!) and minimize your liabilities (we all have them, too!).

Imprinting can be demonstrated easily. When I lead a seminar, I usually enter the room or stage and count out loud to seven. Then we discuss what just happened in the minds of the participants. Without knowing anything about my background, skills, or history, the members of my audience make significant decisions about me.

Research suggests that it's not just one thing that people judge about us in those seven short seconds after meeting us, but at least eleven different factors. These include your:

1. Socioeconomic level
2. Education level
3. Competence and honesty, believability, and perceived credibility
4. Sex role identification
5. Level of sophistication
6. Trustworthiness
7. Level of success
8. Ethnicity
9. Religious background
10. Political background
11. Social / sexual / professional desirability

Different contexts of the first meeting—professional, social, romantic—will rearrange these factors according to varying levels of importance. In the case of Judy, the human resources manager who interviewed Charlie and Roger, she's not supposed to consider sex role identification, ethnicity, religious background, political background, or sexual desirability in her professional imprint of a candidate. These factors need to score zero. But other factors become hugely important, including competence, honesty, believability, credibility, and trustworthiness. Based on her seven-second assessment of the appearances of both Charlie and Roger, according to these five measurements she sorted them into the categories of loser and winner, respectively.

In contrast, if you're introduced to a potential romantic partner, the imprint values will be rearranged. In such a situation, number eleven—social/sexual/professional desirability—will probably leap to the top of the list, along with sex role identification. If the person fails these two tests, nothing else will matter.

And if you bring home your new partner to meet your mother, you know which factor will be number one.... yep, it's probably going to be socioeconomic level (mothers tend to be pragmatic about these things).

🐦 Sylvie di Giusto @Sylvie_diGiusto
"It's not about being someone you're not. It's about affecting others
without saying a word." #TheImageOfLeadership

The Science of First Impressions

There's emerging science that links the seven-second imprint to measurable brain activity. In 2009, neuroscientists at New York University and Harvard University identified the neural systems involved in forming first impressions of others. The findings, which show how we encode social information and then evaluate it in making initial judgments, were reported in the journal *Nature Neuroscience*.

The study was based on the concept that each new person whom we meet presents a set of ambiguous and complex information. Because it's a first meeting, the information is primarily visual, although other senses—hearing, smell, and even touch if you shake hands—can come into play. We quickly sort through this information and judge whether we are attracted to that person or not. It's an ancient and deeply embedded process that allowed our ancestors to quickly assess their relationship to a new person. Friend or foe? Social superior or inferior? And perhaps most significantly, will this person be useful to the group—a leader—or will he or she be a burden and consume more than they contribute?

But how does this complex process happen? The study published in *Nature Neuroscience* sought to investigate the brain mechanisms that give rise to impressions formed immediately after meeting a new person. It was conducted in the laboratory of Elizabeth Phelps, an NYU professor of psychology and neuroscience and one of the co-authors. The study's lead author was Daniela Schiller, a post-doctoral fellow at the Department of Psychology and its Center for Neural Science at NYU.

To explore the process of first impression formation, the researchers designed an experiment in which they examined the brain activity when participants made initial evaluations of fictional individuals. The participants were given written profiles of twenty individuals with different personality traits. The profiles, presented along with pictures of these fictional individuals, included scenarios indicating both positive (e.g., intelligent) and negative (e.g., lazy) traits in their depictions.

After reading the profiles, the participants were asked to evaluate how much they liked or disliked each profiled individual. These impressions varied depending on how much each participant valued the different positive and negative traits conveyed. For instance, if a participant liked intelligence in a partner more than they disliked laziness, he or she might form a positive impression.

During this impression formation period, the brain activity of the participants was observed using functional magnetic resonance imaging (fMRI). Based on the participants' responses, the researchers were able to measure the difference in brain activity when they encountered information that was more, as opposed to less, important in forming the first impression.

During the encoding of impression-relevant information, the neuroimaging results revealed significant activity in two regions of the brain. The first, the posterior cingulate cortex (PCC), has been linked to economic decision-making and assigning subjective value to rewards. The second, the amygdala, is a small structure in the medial temporal lobe that previously has been linked to emotional learning about inanimate objects, as well as social evaluations based on trust or race group. In the study, these parts of the brain showed increased activity when encoding information that was consistent with the impression.

The study suggested that when we only briefly encounter others and have limited and ambiguous cues to evaluate, brain regions that are important in emotional learning and representing value are engaged. When encoding everyday social information during a social encounter, these regions sort information based on its personal and subjective significance, and summarize it into a single value—that is, a first impression made within seven seconds.

Thus, we can say that our emotional learning + our values = the person's imprint.

In training, I encourage my professional clients to evaluate when those first impressions are important for them: Having a job interview as a candidate, performing it as an interviewer, being a possible candidate for a promotion (knowingly or not), meeting the team for the first time, meeting it every day in the morning, presenting at the management board, meeting with clients, meeting vendors and suppliers, representing their brand at a trade show or corporate event. Then I let them decide at which occasions they represent themselves as individuals and when they represent their current employers.

Do you know what? They find out that they always represent both. There is no contact point where it's just about themselves. They always represent their company, even if applying for a job at another company.

🐦 **Sylvie di Giusto @Sylvie_diGiusto**
"As a leader you never represent only yourself, or just your company. You always represent both." #TheImageOfLeadership

The Sustained Imprint

The first impression is only the beginning. It needs to evolve into a lasting positive impression. I call this the "sustained imprint."

I once developed and organized a leadership seminar for a group of twenty high potentials of the retail and tourism company I worked for. The participants were quite surprised to find out that their trainer was not a person; instead, we trained them with the help of horses.

In one of the first exercises we split the participants into two groups. The first group went into the riding area where an unleashed horse was waiting for them. The participants were told to walk in straight with confident steps, to appear strong, to keep eye contact with the horse, and to keep a straight face. When they arrived at the horse they smacked their horsewhips on the ground several times, and the horse immediately began to run in a circle. They whipped and whipped, and they were briefed to stop when the horse appeared to be tired. When they put aside the whip, something "magical" happened—the horse followed them everywhere. They walked around the horse arena and the horse happily trotted after them. None of the participants had said one word to the horse. The horse just followed; obviously it was impressed by the appearance and power of leadership it had experienced.

The second group received a different briefing. They were supposed to walk in and appear friendly and kind to the horse. They were told to motivate the horse by petting it, talking to it, and by developing a relationship. They even brought in treats and encouraged the horse with all their hearts.

The first observation we made was that they had a hard time making the horse run in a circle—it was obvious that the horse wanted more treats and more tender loving care. Finally they were able to make the horse run, but when they dropped their whip, nothing happened. The horse didn't follow, and didn't even come back for more treats, because obviously there were no more treats.

What did we learn? Horses judge you by your appearance and your attitude. The way you appear, the way you look, and the way you make your first impression. What you say to them goes in at one ear and out at the other.

We also learned that the first group celebrated their success, danced around arm-in-arm, and were so confident in their ownership of this horse that they really felt like leaders and winners of this game. But over time, the reality was more complex. Not only did they rest on their laurels, they also became inconsistent in their appearance and their behavior. To the horse, they were no longer predictable. And if there is anything we value in a leader, it's consistency, and that they are predictable in their statements, in their choices, and in the way they appear and react.

The first group didn't keep up with the first impression they left. They were not able to transfer it into a sustained imprint, and the horse paid them back quickly.

This was the reason the two CEOs mentioned at the beginning of the book both failed in the long run. While we were very impressed by their first impressions and followed them for a while without questioning anything, they didn't maintain a sustained imprint. You might say that their success went to their heads, and their image of leadership faded away. If he's not careful, the same could happen to our friend Roger.

The game isn't over after seven seconds. Outstanding leaders leave lasting impressions by how they look and how they present themselves, always and everywhere. Like with the experience of Roger, the positive impression developed in seven seconds only gets you in the door. It makes the possibility of acceptance very real. It breaks down the barrier between you and your audience or the person you meet. Conversely, the negative impression that Charlie created caused the door to slam shut. It reduced the possibility of acceptance and created a barrier between him and his audience—who in this case was just one person, and that one person

🐦 **Mark LaPenna**
@MarkLaPenna

"A first impression will gain you an invite, a lasting impression will assure you are asked back."

#TheImageOfLeadership

had the power to either help him up the ladder of success or pass him by in favor of someone else.

You'll recall that Charlie and Roger had résumés that were identical. (This is not hypothetical; in today's competitive job marketplace, among dozens of qualified applicants for a given position there are bound to be several candidates who look the same on paper.) The chances are good that when Judy first met them and they had a conversation—that is, during the first seven seconds—there wasn't much difference in the actual words they spoke. If you were to read a written transcript of both interviews, the first pages might be hard to distinguish.

There's a famous study by Albert Mehrabian that suggests that the words that you say—the *actual words*, not the tone or inflection—account for only seven percent of the imprint that you make. It's called the 7%-38%-55% rule, where words account for seven percent, tone of voice accounts for 38 percent, and body language accounts for 55 percent of the imprint you make. The focus of this study was on some very specific areas of communication and doesn't precisely correlate to real-world conditions. Yet some image consultants and trainers use this study to suggest it's not important what you say or how you behave, it's only about the appearance. Of course that's just not true.

However, if you have only seven seconds to make an excellent first impression, your appearance takes on greater importance. Many people do not even have the chance to use their behavior and communication for a powerful first impression. Think of politicians or even CEOs of big companies. Most ordinary people never have the chance to actually meet them and to experience their behavior and to discuss certain issues with them. In most cases they only know these people from pictures. So what's left, other than their appearance?

We've all heard about the historic television debates held in 1960 between the two candidates for president of the United States, Richard M. Nixon and John F. Kennedy. The series of four encounters were the first televised debates in history. On the day of the first debate, Nixon was campaigning until just a few hours before the cameras rolled, and in the studio he refused makeup. As a result his beard stubble showed prominently on the era's black-and-white TV screens. Kennedy, by contrast, who was well rested and had prepared extensively beforehand, appeared tanned, confident, and relaxed. An estimated seventy million viewers watched the first debate. In terms of content—that is, the *actual words* said by each candidate—the judgment of history is uncertain. But what is certain is that people who watched the debate on television overwhelmingly believed Kennedy had won, while the smaller, more rural radio audience believed Nixon had won. After the first debate, polls showed Kennedy moving from a slight deficit into a slight lead over Nixon. The viewers saw Kennedy as a leader and a winner, and responded accordingly.

The principles are still true today. In a visual-driven world, those details count more and more. It's not a coincidence that Bill de Blasio shaved off his beard when running for the office of mayor of New York City against Joe Lhota. According to a survey by the online newspaper *amNewYork*, just three men who have occupied City Hall since 1913 have had facial hair. While it seems to be a detail for us, it's an important decision a political leader has to make. Is the beard a distraction? Is it worth risking that people or press will discuss it? De Blasio knew that visual impressions matter to voters, and he went with what he knew would be a readily accepted look.

🐦 Sylvie di Giusto @Sylvie_DiGiusto

"Outstanding leaders leave lasting impressions by how they look & how they present themselves, always & everywhere." #TheImageOfLeadership

Confirmation Bias

If you mess it up with your appearance, it's much harder to get back on track by behavioral and communicative excellence. Complicating matters is the fact that *confirmation bias* compels the audience to *ignore* any signs that go against their first impressions. In contrast, they are extremely sensitive to signs or indicators that *support* their initial take on the type of person you are.

In the Kennedy-Nixon debates I just mentioned, during debates two, three, and four, which were all televised, Nixon was well rested and wore appropriate studio makeup. Political experts agree that he won the second and third debates, and that the fourth debate was a draw. But the television audience had dwindled for these debates, and unfortunately for Nixon much of the electorate had already developed a confirmation bias: Nixon was the ragged one, while Kennedy was the one who was alert, clean-cut, and looked more like a leader.

Confirmation bias is a powerful force that's used in marketing. Let's say, for example, that you've never seen Miley Cyrus. All you know is that she's some sort of popular singer. At the same time, someone tells you to check out another singer—let's say it's the great opera star Renée Fleming.

Your friend shows you two photos, one of Renée Fleming and one of Miley Cyrus. Your friend then provides a brief one-sentence description of each performer, and asks you to match the description with the photo. Unless you've been living under a rock, you'd be able to do this instantly. This is because both Miley Cyrus and Renée Fleming are scrupulous about the respective images they project to the public. They use confirmation bias to reinforce our intuitive first impressions of them. Once you believe, for example, that Miley Cyrus is wild and uninhibited, you'll assume that just about anything she does is a reflection of her wild and uninhibited attitude. The message is conveyed by her total imprint: clothes, hair, makeup, attitude, song lyrics, dance moves. Her manager, Larry Rudolph (who, by the way, also manages Miley's cultural predecessor Britney Spears, so he's had plenty of practice doing this sort of thing), takes the necessary steps to ensure that Miley's public wild-child persona is both vivid and consistent.

It's as simple as that. If the person you meet sees a stain on your shirt or on your dress, they will look for evidence in your behavior and your communication that will reinforce the evidence provided by the stain that you are sloppy in your work style. It's just an unnecessary distraction you bring to the table that can easily be avoided.

> **Heidi Deblaere @hdeblaere**
> "Image isn't just a surface issue. Your image is strongly tied to your effectiveness as a leader."
> #TheImageOfLeadership

On the other hand, if the person you meet forms the impression that you are well groomed, dressed appropriately, and exude confidence, they'll gladly take additional information—the words that you say, for example—and fit it against the model they have formed in their mind that you are a leader. If the new information matches, the effects of confirmation bias are multiplied in your favor.

> **Sylvie di Giusto @Sylvie_diGiusto**
> "Confirmation bias compels the audience to ignore any signs that go against their first impressions." #TheImageOfLeadership

Stand Out for the Right Reasons

I mentioned earlier that Roger's motivation for excellence in his professional imprint was not vanity but humility. His goal is to make those around him relaxed and confident, and to blend seamlessly with the team. This is without a doubt the most effective way to get hired for a position.

This does not mean that Roger is a wallflower or that he is bland. Far from it—he shines like a star. The fact is that in today's business world, the vast majority of people—even successful people—are merely average in their appearance. They wear average suits, have average haircuts, put on average shoes, and say average things. They have average ideas and average expectations. When someone like Judy needs to conduct interviews for a position, chances are she'll have to sort through a stack of average résumés and talk to a bunch of candidates who all sound and look the same.

Because every aspect of Roger's appearance is of the highest quality and reflects his best qualities—the cut of his clothing, the color, the line, the workmanship—he stands out from the crowd. To Judy, who every day sees an endless procession of lukewarm boring candidates, Roger is like a beacon of light. He cuts through the clutter and gets noticed—and remembered.

The look of leadership is—and will always be—the exception, not the rule. This book could be a *New York Times* best seller, and the world would still be full of gray people with oatmeal ideas. So have no fear. Your job is to be the very best that you can be, and if you do this, success will find its way to your door.

I know what you're thinking: Is it always good to stand out? For Miley Cyrus, standing out from the crowd in any way that she can will always bring positive returns. Whatever gets her mentioned in the press will help her sell records. For an entertainer like her, standing out from the crowd, regardless of the reason, is good. If she gets on the evening news simply because everybody thinks she has done something awful, she's won the game.

But in the professional universe, standing out for its own sake is a terrible idea. In the pro-

🐦 **Cassandra B. Jackson
@DCCooky**

"Don't take work attire advice from Hollywood. Too short. Too tight. Too low." #TheImageOfLeadership

The Image of Leadership by Sylvie di Giusto

fessional space, there's a *good* way to stand out and there's a *bad* way to stand out.

The good way to stand out is to do two things: Be your very best self, and exemplify the highest values of your organization.

The bad way is... well, it's any other way.

I know a woman who rose to the level of middle manager in her company. Gina was highly intelligent and her job performance was as good as anyone's. She also dressed well and was always well groomed. There was absolutely nothing about her that detracted from anyone's ability or inclination to view her as a leader, whether at first glance or over time.

Well—almost nothing. For some reason that I will never understand, Gina insisted upon wearing eyeglasses that were too small for her face. The frames were made of wire and the lenses were set close together. The overall effect was that this perfectly wonderful woman looked like a rodent dressed in a pantsuit. I actually had co-workers take me aside and say, "Do you know why Gina wears those peculiar glasses?" I think that Gina thought the glasses made her look "distinctive." The fact is that the glasses were a huge distraction. They made her look like a loser, not a winner. Despite the glasses, she was able to rise to a certain level in the company. But eventually she hit the ceiling and didn't get any higher.

I've seen unfortunate people stand out from the crowd for all sorts of reasons: strange hairstyles, weird facial hair (on men, that is!), dresses that are too tight (why, oh why, do so many women do this?), grotesque fingernails, huge eyelashes, suffocating perfume, plunging décolletage, gigantic hunks of jewelry.... the list goes on and on.

These are the kinds of things that will make someone like Judy think, "Oh yes, I remember her. She was the one whose hair was loaded with greasy gel. Ugh! No way is she going to work here!"

I was once put in charge of finding the new executive assistant for the CEO of our company, which had one hundred thousand employees. Since I was also responsible for a development program we created especially for the specific needs of executive assistants, I had a pretty clear and deep insight into the skills and experience levels of the top assistants who were the most reputable and prestigious within the group. I found her—the perfect candidate. A lovely young ambitious woman who at that time worked for one of the managing directors. She had everything the CEO was asking for, and on paper, based on her skills and experience, she was indeed the best possible choice. Certain of success, I presented her resume to my boss, the management board member responsible for human resources. To my amazement he declined her.

Although he made an effort to cite formal reasons and clarifications, he randomly mentioned her fingernails. He mentioned it as if it were something that was not relevant to his decision, but obviously it was relevant enough to mention it to me. I indeed remembered she had extra-long, yellowish, non-manicured nails. They were unattractive and seemed unhygienic.

I knew him well enough to understand he wouldn't point it out if it hadn't been relevant to his decision, and of course I thought to myself: Is it fair? Is it right to deny her advancement because of her fingernails? Of course it isn't. But try to step back and see the case from the perspective of the CEO. How often would this CEO be confronted with those fingernails? Every time she pointed out the button on the screen where he has to click, every time she showed him the email he was supposed to read, every time she flipped through the contracts he had to sign and pointed to the line where he had to write his signature, every time she showed him his departure time on the ticket, every time she handed over his bag and shook his hand before leaving... I could list hundreds of occasions this CEO would have been distracted by those fingernails on a daily basis. And while it might be only a small detail for you and me, it quite possibly could be important for someone else.

We never told her. Years later I met her again. Of course, she had still the same fingernails. I was hoping that someone else would have given her an opportunity to showcase her excellent skills. However, as long as she has worked for this company she never got promoted.

🐦 **Fatima Sheikh @FSCharlie**
"You'll never seek the opportunities you never knew you had."
#TheImageOfLeadership

Leaders understand and accept that it's about the details. Those little details can make us stand out for both the right and the wrong reasons. Those details will be of different importance from person to person.

It's something I stress in my corporate trainings. For example, if you work for an airline and spend most of your time behind the check-in counter getting passengers ready for their flights, your clean and shiny shoes are important. But they do not have the relevance that your makeup and hair have, because most passengers spend their time staring at you over the counter while you check them in for their flight. The impression you leave on their mind is an impression they will take on the flight and on their way home. Their memory is vivid when they book the next flight with your airline—or not.

One jarring detail can be enough to get you consigned to the category of loser—or create an unwanted distraction, as we can see for example when we take a close look at the neckties worn by the current president of the United States.

On June 19, 2013, as President Barack Obama stepped to the podium in Berlin, he wore what has become his trademark blue tie. In his speech, the most powerful person in the world proposed a cooling of the arms race and the reduction of both America's and Russia's nuclear arsenals by one-third.

The choice of a blue tie was no accident. Presidential style watchers know that when appearing in public, President Obama usually only wears either a blue tie or a red one. Considering that even the slightest variation matters if we are talking about the president of the United States, what is the reasoning behind red and blue ties?

The emphasis in Washington D.C. is on fitting in, not on standing out. And when it comes to business and high-stakes politics, only two colors of men's neckties are universally acceptable: red and blue. There are the occasional yellow ties, but these are regarded as idiosyncratic and are worn by people who insist upon being perceived as highly individualistic. (Billionaire real estate developer Donald Trump wears yellow, purple, and even pink ties, which tends to prove the point. And there was a time in the mid-1980s when yellow neckties were all the rage. Fortunately, that fad went the way of padded shoulders and hair gel.) Purple is beginning to be seen as a "nonpartisan" color among newscasters who don't want to wear either red (Republican) or blue (Democratic). Red and blue are thought to improve receptivity to advertising and increase brain performance. This makes sense when the president is trying to convey a message to his audience, those subtle nuances may subconsciously be working. If there is any group of people on the planet who love to gain advantages, it has to be politicians. Neckties play their part in accomplishing that.

If President Obama were about to deliver a serious speech with implications, something that he wanted his audience to understand, to present himself as an authority figure, and if he were trying speak to the nation rather than engage in a discussion, he would likely wear red. Perhaps his most famous example in the first term came when announcing the death of Osama Bin Laden. President Obama addressed the nation with a red tie.

Also interesting to note is that when seen together, President Obama and Vice-President Joe Biden appear to coordinate efforts. They make sure to wear alternating necktie colors so as not to duplicate each other.

As the president stood in Berlin, blue allowed him to come across as seeking peace. This may be especially important when standing in front of an international crowd and making an appeal to the world. Everything about his behavior during that event came across as open, as though he wanted the world to hear him—from removing his jacket (appearing less formal) to chewing bubble gum.

Whenever you see President Obama wearing his red or blue tie, keep in mind that his choice that day is not accidental. For a high-profile leader, these details are extremely important, and one idiosyncratic choice can become an unwelcome distraction.

🐦 **Sylvie di Giusto @Sylvie_diGiusto**
"The look of leadership is the exception, not the rule.
You've to stand out, but for the right reasons." #TheImageOfLeadership

The ABCDs of Your Professional Imprint

Your professional imprint is the sum total of four factors: your appearance, behavior, communication, and your digital footprint. Here's an easy way to remember these four key elements of your professional imprint—just think of ABCD.

APPEARANCE includes every visual element that can be seen and understood in the first seven seconds: your physical fitness (or lack thereof), your hair and nails, your suit and shoes, your posture, your eye contact. In any situation where you have only one chance to quickly impress another person—it could be an interviewer, your new boss, a recent addition to your team, or a potential client—it's important to ensure that you create the best first impression. Before you ever utter a word, the other person is going to look at your clothes and immediately decide whether you have dressed appropriately for this occasion. If you show up looking like you got dressed in the dark (for example, a rumpled shirt for men), the chances are good that the other person is going to apply that perception elsewhere. Perhaps they'll assume that you have a sloppy working style, and that paying attention to details is not your strong suit.

Our appearance is a form of nonverbal communication, and one that speaks very loudly.

BEHAVIOR includes the sum total of your actions. It's your *attitude*. A leader is an individual who has earned the respect of others and who leads them effectively and in the right direction. Leadership is able to inspire at all times, and the key to this is attitude. A leader's attitude evokes positive feelings in people.

Effective leaders use influence to orient others towards their goals. Being a good leader is less about being the smartest and more about understanding others and what makes a team work together to reach solutions. Personality is central to the workplace; depending on their personalities, people come together in harmony or in conflict, and tensions can easily be caused. The best leaders will harness the strengths and skills that people have and use them to their best abilities, meeting the demands of the workplace.

Leadership has been described by *Forbes* as a marathon rather than a short sprint. As the workplace becomes more flexible, diverse and mobile than ever before, leaders need to adapt to the changes and see them in a positive light. The best leaders inspire their teams to work hard on a long-term basis.

The visionary leader inspires through exciting ideas, and their teams follow them and are motivated by their enthusiasm and knowledge. The empathetic leader relates well to others, and is able to relate to and understand their experiences. The ethical leader abides by rules about behavior, with every employee adhering to these rules and the workplace becoming a moral environment.

Whether they inspire their team by providing a sympathetic ear or by setting a positive example, a good attitude helps a leader reach those goals and ultimately win over others. Armed with a positive attitude, you can rally your staff around you and reward them when they reach their goals.

Great leaders listen to their staff and understand how to make the workplace a happier, as well as more productive, environment. Leaders with positive attitudes find that their followers appreciate the personal connection, whether it's through empathy, vision or reward systems, and that ultimately people respond much better to someone who empowers them.

COMMUNICATION is sharing information and ideas between individuals or groups to reach a common understanding. With so many personalities, ideas, and an overload of information in the workplace, effective communication is a challenge for business owners, CEOs, managers, and employees. Effective communication is a business tool and essential employee attribute. A company knows that in order for its objectives to be met, communication is the key to success. Communication links and facilitates all aspects of a company. When all members of a team, department, and workplace communicate effectively together, then productivity increases, a better workplace environment is created, and objectives are met more efficiently.

Communication is not only important in the workplace, but for the company when dealing with partners, clients, and vendors. The way you communicate sets a precedent for the company; therefore, your communication needs to be clear, persuasive, and concise. If you can learn to openly and effectively communicate, you will set yourself apart and opportunities will come your way more frequently. Fortunately, effective communication is a skill that can be learned.

You are there because you will contribute to the organization's growth and provide leadership to your colleagues. Everything you say and do must confirm what your colleagues or audience members have decided in those first seven seconds: that you are a winner and a potential leader.

DIGITAL FOOTPRINT. This is how you present yourself on the Internet. As we move into the twenty-first century, this factor that once existed only in science fiction is becoming increasingly important. Like it or not, the Internet and social media provide new avenues for both advancing your professional imprint and for incurring damage to your reputation. Your online digital reputation has never been more important. While years ago much of our personal information was considered private, today our digital reputations expose more information about our lives than ever before, and information about almost all adult Americans can be found online. Your online digital reputation defines how people perceive you without ever having a single conversation with you. The fact is, a digital reputation can be incorrect, it may present only partial information, and it might even allow for slander and online attacks to define us for others.

The Image of Leadership by Sylvie di Giusto

The Internet consolidates information about you, your family, your friends, and your business, and delivers that information through a simple search query. This information can have a lasting presence online, permanently impacting you. Exposure of this private digital information can profoundly influence whether or not you land a new job or get a promotion.

Be proactive about protecting your digital reputation. Once a reputation is tarnished it's almost impossible to make it shine again. Check your digital reputation by searching for all the variations of your name; each will offer potentially different search results.

As you review your online digital reputation, make sure that your findings reflect the reputation you'd like to share with the world, with current and future employers, colleagues, friends, and family members. Remember that your online reputation can be a determining factor for hiring or being offered that important initial interview.

Look at your internet profile as a second self, the one you want everyone to know in addition to your real self. Just as you use office etiquette in the workplace and save your rougher side for watching the football game, take time to distinguish your online reputation from how you may behave in private. Your online reputation should say what you want it to say and no more. And I'm aware it's a fine line. Having no personal information on Google can be just as damaging as having inappropriate content.

🐦 **Sylvie di Giusto @Sylvie_diGiusto**

"Your professional imprint is the sum total of your appearance, behavior, communication, and your digital footprint." #TheImageOfLeadership

Executive Presence

Every detail of your ABCD—appearance, behavior, communication, and digital footprint—adds up to your professional imprint.

Your professional imprint needs to be positive. It needs to create the aura of executive presence. It's a feeling of leadership and confidence that you inspire in everyone with whom you come into contact.

According to a 2012 report issued by the Center for Talent Innovation (CTI), based on a survey of nearly four thousand college-educated professionals, leadership roles are given to people who exude executive presence, which is defined as individuals who look and act like leaders.

Promotions are not just a function of skills and aptitude, the CTI report revealed. Executive presence is "a required yet unwritten" competency for leaders. The survey found that male and female senior executives who participated in the survey estimated that executive presence constitutes one-quarter of what it takes to get promoted.

🐦 **Sarah Hathorn**
@sarahhathorn
"Executive Presence is leveraging your personal style to influence your audience."
#TheImageOfLeadership

Executive presence is made up of three distinct qualities: gravitas, communication, and appearance. Gravitas is communicated by the way you speak and act, and signals to colleagues that you're someone worthy of being heard and followed. Communication involves the ability to speak directly, and to convey not only the substance of your ideas, but a sense that you should be listened to. Appearance "opens the door and gets you invited in," the CTI found. Good grooming—looking polished and put together—mattered most to the survey's respondents. The survey found that 83 percent of senior executives believe that "unkempt attire" detracts from a woman's executive presence, while 75 percent of senior execs believe it detracts from a man's.

🐦 **Sylvie di Giusto @Sylvie_DiGiusto**
"Your professional imprint needs to be positive. It needs to create the aura of executive presence." #TheImageOfLeadership

Internal and External Consistency

For leaders, consistency is key. What I'm talking about is your *internal* professional imprint and your *external* professional imprint, and how they work together.

Your internal professional imprint is how you appear, behave, and communicate within the closed universe of your company and your colleagues. This means at meetings, working with peers, reporting to your boss or to the board, and supervising subordinates. We've all seen the insincere colleague who flatters his boss while behaving rudely to subordinates. These people don't last very long because they are displaying poor leadership skills—and leaders are chosen, not born. You don't get to be a leader unless enough of your peers give their consent.

Your external imprint is how you appear as a representative of your company to stakeholders, clients, financiers, talk-show audiences, the local chamber of commerce—anyone or any group who might do business with, or interact with, your company.

These dual imprints must be consistent and must position you as a leader.

There are always those who, in a misguided effort to find an easy path that will allow them to ignore these fundamental truths, will point to the spectacular career of the late Steve Jobs. He was one of those very few exceptions that prove the rule. In 1976, Steve Jobs, Steve Wozniak, and Ronald Wayne formed Apple Computer in the garage of Jobs's parents' house. Wayne soon left, leaving Jobs and Wozniak as the primary co-founders of the company. What this means is that Steve Jobs didn't have to apply for a job, and his public persona was always closer to that of a mad inventor rather than a conventional CEO. While Jobs was a persuasive and charismatic director for Apple, many of his employees from that time described him as an erratic and difficult manager. Jobs notoriously kept meetings running past midnight, sent out lengthy overnight faxes, and then called new meetings at seven the next morning. In the early 1980s, disappointing sales caused a deterioration in Jobs's working relationship with Apple CEO Mike Sculley, which devolved into a power struggle between the two.

On May 24, 1985, Sculley called a board meeting, during which Jobs was removed from his managerial duties as head of the Macintosh division. He resigned from Apple five months later.

Eleven years later, in 1996, Apple announced that it would bring Jobs back to the company he co-founded. Jobs became de facto chief in September 1997, and he—and the company—never looked back.

Make no mistake: Steve Jobs carefully cultivated his internal and external imprints. Ask yourself whether you ever saw him appear in anything other than jeans and a black turtleneck. No, you did not. The late Apple co-founder was best known for his visionary leadership and innovation, but he was also known for his unvarying signature look. Unlike most corporate executives who wear suits and ties, Jobs was dedicated to his chosen uniform of a black mock turtleneck, blue jeans, and New Balance sneakers.

Participants in my training seminars sometimes offer the idea that they too can be successful by copying this signature look. I tell them straightforwardly, "No you can't!" Why not? they ask. "Because you didn't invent a computer in your garage." Simply said, because you are not Steve Jobs.

You also have to consider that self-made entrepreneurs like Steve Jobs don't have to apply for jobs like our friends Charlie and Roger do. And, by the way, there are plenty of pictures showing Steve Jobs dressed in a suit when he was a young entrepreneur and he was reaching out to banks.

Furthermore, why would you want to be like somebody else? Choose to be the best you can be. Commit to yourself, and don't compare yourself to anyone else. Famous business people and politicians are known to be consistent with their wardrobe because it's their brand identity. It's who they are, how they want to represent themselves, and it makes the statement that it's not about what you wear but what you accomplish.

> **Jessica Kupferman**
> **@JessKupferman**
>
> "You can't ever be the next so-and-so. You can only be the first one of your kind. Own it!"
> #TheImageOfLeadership

Facebook founder Mark Zuckerberg, for instance, wears casual clothing to the office because he represents the entire generation of young people who don't want to wear suits to work. On NBC's *Today* show, he said, "I mean, I wear the same thing every day, right? I mean, it's literally, if you could see my closet, I own maybe about twenty grey shirts"—the ones for which he is famous. "I have one drawer," Zuckerberg said. "Like men everywhere." In 2011 he was named to the worst dressed lists of both GQ and Esquire.

He's also worth over twelve billion dollars, so he can dress however he wants. But he knows when to step up his game. While it's obviously okay for him to meet and greet his guests, whoever they are, in this more or less very casual work attire, he does understand that he has to dress up when he's not on his turf. At his wedding—luckily—there are photos showing him in a suit. When visiting the president of the United States you'll indeed find him wearing a suit and a tie. Is it the traditional suit we both might think it has to be? No, it's not. It's very much Mark Zuckerberg's interpretation of a suit, and a dress code that's a) appropriate for meeting the president of the United States and b) that doesn't distract from the important things those two had to discuss, to decide or to present to the public, which would obviously happen if he stood there in his grey t-shirt.

Entrepreneurs like Steve Jobs and Mark Zuckerberg wear what they wear because that's what they feel comfortable wearing, they feel confident, and it's also useful to have a trademark look. It makes them memorable and distinctive. It eliminates the necessity of deciding what to wear every day. President Barack Obama is another good example of a powerful person who dresses pragmatically—he once said in an interview with Vanity Fair that the reason he wears only grey and blue suits is, "You need to focus your decision-making energy. You need to routinize yourself."

Whatever your professional imprint is, make sure that it's consistent and that it reinforces the perception that you are a leader.

🐦 Sylvie di Giusto @Sylvie_diGiusto

"Make sure your professional imprint is consistent and that it reinforces the perception that you are a leader." #TheImageOfLeadership

Chapter 3
Leaders Look Confident

🐦 **Dawn Gallagher**
@YourHomeSpa
"True leaders know the secret
to success is appreciating
what you have while working
towards what you want."
#TheImageOfLeadership

What is confidence, what does it mean to look confident, and why would it matter for a leader? It is indeed a complex question.

I'm going to start exploring it by talking about acting and actors, and the methods they use to create believable characters. Let's say you're an actor and you've been hired to play the part of someone who is a leader— say, Joan of Arc or King Henry VIII. You need to look like the leader and you need the audience to believe your portrayal.

🐦 **Nikk Smit**
@NikkBishopSmit
"Confidence is that silent humming force that beams. Yes, yes, yes, you can do it. You have what it takes."
#TheImageOfLeadership

One way of getting into the character might be called the classical approach, where you begin by studying the exterior qualities of your character. You analyze their clothes, learn their physical appearance and body type, and imitate their mannerisms. In a sense, you work from the outside in. The idea is that if you diligently assume the external attributes of a leader, you'll become a convincing leader.

The other way, loosely called the method acting approach, is to study the inner psychology of your character. Who was Joan of Arc? What was she trying to accomplish? What was she afraid of, and how would these apprehensions manifest themselves in her behavior? And, oh yes, she needs to wear a suit of armor too, but that's the easy part. In this approach, you work from the inside out. The idea is that if you think and feel like a leader, and master their internal attributes, you'll become a convincing leader. You won't be "acting"; you'll inhabit the part.

Does that mean you can just dress up in a suit and it will make you leadership material, both in your eyes and in the eyes of others? Can you fake it 'til you make it? No, certainly not. It's simply that the chances are much greater that you'll appear, behave, communicate and perceive yourself as a leader in a "power suit"

🐦 **Mallory Sills @MallorySills**
"Even if you're not feeling confident, dress in a way that shows confidence. Your state of mind will follow." #TheImageOfLeadership

than in a grey shirt and flip-flops. It's an instrument you can use on your way to become a leader. Don't fake it 'til you make it. Instead, fake it 'til you really become it.

To look like a leader at work and in your community, I want you to use both techniques. I want you to work on your interior and your exterior simultaneously. Get the inside figured out, and at the same time upgrade the outside.

If you *look* like a leader, it will be easier for you to *feel* like a leader.

And if you *feel* like a leader, then *looking* like one will seem to be a natural extension of your personality.

🐦 **Sylvie di Giusto @Sylvie_diGiusto**
"If you look like a leader, it will be easier for you to feel like a leader."
#TheImageOfLeadership

Start with Your Birthday Suit

Let's start our discussion about confidence by ignoring all the stuff you can buy at a department store, and talk about the outfit you were born with.

When talking about this with my clients, most of them agree that confidence begins with your attitude towards the body you inhabit. Tall or short, fat or lean, old or young, a confident person works with the body he or she has. Confident people don't complain about their body issues; they take their body the exact way it is and either work with it or change the body issues. They seem to have no insecurities, and instead they know how to stand out for all the right reasons.

🐦 **Megan Brandle @MegsImageGuide**
"Disregard your age/body/gender and take time to be grateful for the wonderful person you are."
#TheImageOfLeadership

I'd like to approach the subject from my own professional experience. People might assume that most of my clients hire me in anticipation of a certain occasion—a job interview, promotion, career change, political campaign, public speaking event— and they need to prepare. The truth is that while many clients very often use one of these occasions to hire me, it turns out the true reason or the challenge they are facing is that they are very doubtful about themselves and are burdened by low self-esteem. This self-doubt is very often related to their body (weight and height), their age (young and old), or their gender (sometimes including sexuality).

As image consultants, we provide our valued clients with tips and tricks on how to appear one or two inches taller or shorter, one or two sizes thinner or heavier, one or two years older or younger, or one or two teeny-tiny tricks to look more or less feminine. But I also stress that you cannot change the fundamentals: someone short will never be tall, someone overweight will never look skinny, and a woman should never try to look like a man. Instead, it's more important that you are confident about your body, age, and gender. Otherwise, all those tips and tricks won't work anyway.

Start with loving yourself. And love yourself just a little bit more than everybody else does.

> **Brandy Hartman**
> **@BrandyLotusgirl**
> "Confidence is knowing and loving oneself, but also accepting one's own limitations. No one is perfect."
> #TheImageOfLeadership

> **Sylvie di Giusto @Sylvie_diGiusto**
> "Confidence begins with your attitude towards the body you inhabit."
> #TheImageOfLeadership

Leaders Are Confident About Their Bodies

While confidence comes from inside, the easiest way to show it is with your exterior appearance. Aside from ethnicity and gender, your exterior appearance is primarily influenced by two factors: your height and your weight. A study by Sylvia Ann Hewlett at Center for Talent Innovation of more than four thousand college-educated professionals and 268 senior executives surveyed executive presence. In this study, researchers found that women are judged more critically by their weight, but men are more likely to be judged by their height. Of those surveyed, sixteen percent said it's important for men to be tall, compared to just six percent for women.

Honestly, these results pretty much represent my client base. More women tend to have issues with their weight, and very often ask me to help them with looking thinner. My male clients more often ask me about ways they can look taller. Sometimes, I simply wish they would be more concerned about their health and not so much about their weight or height. The ultimate example of being confident in your own skin is the remarkable election of Barack Obama to the highest office in the United States. Setting aside his qualifications, let's think about his physical appearance, and go back to when he first announced his candidacy for president on February 10, 2007. At that time he was a first-term United States senator who was virtually unknown outside of his home state of Illinois. Ethnically, he was half white and half African-American, and self-identified as black. He was six-foot-one inches tall, which is about average for a modern US president (the tallest were Abraham Lincoln and Lyndon Johnson, each at six feet four inches). His weight was a relatively slender 180 pounds, which gave him one of the lowest body mass indexes of any president (the skinniest president was James Madison, who was five-foot-four inches tall and weighed a scant 122 pounds). Barack Obama was forty-five years old; when he took office in 2009 he was forty-seven, making him the fifth-youngest president in US history (the youngest was Theodore Roosevelt, who took office at age forty-two).

To recap, Barack Obama—whose first name comes from the Swahili word for "one who is blessed"—entered the brutal and high-stakes arena of American presidential politics as a young, skinny black man with no national political platform.

In February of 2007 he could have easily looked at himself in the mirror and said, "Me? Become president of the United States? No way! Maybe I'll wait a few years. I'll look more distinguished. I'll have more gravitas. And anyway, Hillary deserves to get the nomination." Yet to the millions of voters who eventually saw him and heard him, he conveyed the instant and indelible imprint of a leader.

It all began with his confidence in himself. Not hubris or vanity, but the simple belief that what he wanted was both possible and within his grasp.

🐦 **Ranbir Puar @ranbirpuar**

"Your head may create your world, but your body carries it around. Take good care of it!" #TheImageOfLeadership

🐦 **Sylvie di Giusto @Sylvie_diGiusto**

"While confidence comes from inside, the most powerful way to show it is through your exterior appearance." #TheImageOfLeadership

The Irrelevance of Body Shapes

Everyone has some aspects to their body that are pleasing, and some that are not so pleasing. You have to know your body and be honest with yourself. No matter how tall or small, how thin or thick it is, you have to understand your body. Where are the parts you like? And where are those you don't like?

How you think about your body is important. Many image consultants talk about body shapes. They categorize clients into different physical groups, and give their shapes hilarious names such as apples, pears, and bananas.

I do not work with those shapes at all. First of all, who wants to be a full moon? And second, these categories absolutely fail because the requirements of a pear-shaped woman have nothing to do with a pear-shaped man; it depends on how much you would like to show your pear or not, and if you are a petite pear or tall pear changes the story too. I encourage my participants to not get hung up on hilarious names from anyone, and instead to analyze their body in terms of:

1. Where are the positives, and how to highlight them to make you feel confident?

2. Where are the negatives, and how to hide them to make you feel confident?

Let me explain it with my own body. (It's okay—I usually do this in front of a group, so please feel free to use your imagination!). I'm female, taller than average, relatively thin, with long legs and wide shoulders. I do not have a well-defined waist, and like many women (and men) I have a little belly that I just can't make flat. If a traditional image consultant would inspect me, I would be an "inverted triangle" in their opinion. Since I am already quite tall they would tell me to *not* wear high heels, and not to make my lower body part longer and taller, since it already is.

With apologies to all the experts, I do exactly the opposite of what's written in their books. I wear high-waisted pants and high heels that accentuate my legs. I mean, I have damn hot legs—I'd better show them, shouldn't I? They make me feel confident, and that's how leaders feel.

There's a practical reason too. I work with many male clients, and some of them are taller than average. I want to stand at eye level with them, and therefore I wear heels, even if it's not recommended given my body shape. On the other hand, if I'm working with someone who is petite, I don't wear high heels because I don't want to make the other person feel uncomfortable. The occasion is the key! Certainly not the body shape.

Making yourself feel confident is so much more important than any body shape, proportion, or structure that others might talk you into.

🐦 **Beth Bores @bethbores**

"Don't wear clothes that detract from your appearance, either by highlighting a problem or make you look unbalanced." #TheImageOfLeadership

With body types and body parts, there isn't a one-size-fits-all structure you can put people in, that will make them feel more confident about their bodies. What they have to do is understand their body and their options for creating "imprint illusions."

An imprint illusion is where you "manage" what people see by drawing their eyes to certain places. If they're looking at your eyes, for example, they may not notice your big ears. If they're looking at your fabulous legs, they may not notice your small bust. If they're looking at your warm smile, they won't notice that maybe you should lose twenty pounds.

🐦 **Sylvie di Giusto @Sylvie_diGiusto**

"Making yourself feel confident is more important than any body shape or proportion, that others might talk you into." #TheImageOfLeadership

Free Yourself from Color Themes

While we're talking about useless body categories like pears and bananas, the same syndrome is true for color themes. Many image consultants group their clients into categories like "warm autumns" and "cold winters." This is an oversimplification. First of all, it's very possible that you're in one color group depending on the place and climate you were born in. Simply said, people from Africa or South America can often wear yellow, while people of Asian descent often look terrible in yellow.

Furthermore, it makes a difference whether you wear those colors close to your face or at your legs. Your color profile changes while you age. Last but not least—and most importantly—those color themes stand in no relation at all to your industry, your position, your career, the given requirements of your job, and again the occasion.

As always, occasion is key. I'm reminded of my client Jasper—thirty-five years old (according to his driver's license) but looking twenty-five, very tall, lively, and constantly giggling—who stands in front of me in a bright lemon yellow shirt, grass green pants, and orange loafers. Every individual item is within his supposed color theme. He tells me that everybody in the office thinks he is "everybody's darling, always happy, always looking on the bright side of life," and yet he's been passed over for promotions because they have the feeling he's not "serious enough," not "there yet." Jasper is a corporate lawyer, and that always-happy, always-looking-on-the-bright-side-of-life attitude is not the characteristic that people look for in a lawyer. The opposite is true—we expect them to be serious, right?

If someone were to tell me to wear light, bright rose because it's in my color theme, I would not recommend doing that if you are a young female leader who faces the challenge that everyone thinks you're always nice, cute, small, unseen, and invisible. If someone were to tell me to wear white because it's in my color theme—well, it's one of the worst things to do when you're on stage or in front of a camera. And if you work in healthcare or as a social worker, that head-to-toe black outfit doesn't seem to be very approachable for others.

Last but not least, let's not forget those employees who do not have a choice because they have to wear uniforms. You think that is rare? Think again. Department stores, security companies, hospitals and airlines do not care if charcoal makes their people look pale or dreary, or if it's not in your color theme. What they care about is consistency and professionalism in their employees' appearance, and their staff just has to make it work. And let's just be honest, there's also an unspoken uniform in finance and law, where suit colors that depart from navy, charcoal, or black are the exception.

Instead of thinking in color themes, use color for your advantage. There are indeed colors you might look better with, and you should wear them close to your face. But make sure those colors match the requirements of your industry, your job, or the occasion. Just because it's neon pink, you should think about the risk of being the only neon-pink dressed lawyer in the room. Furthermore, if

> 🐦 **Laura Algueró**
> **@mypershopper**
> "Always find the best moment to wear a risky outfit."
> #TheImageOfLeadership

those baggy hips are the parts of your body you do not adore, why would you point them out and draw everyone's attention to them by wearing a pair of red pants? Skip them for the pair of black pants, and wear red on top, so everyone sees your beautiful neck and shoulders.

Furthermore, use color carefully. A great way is to use accessories with colors. Jewelry, ties, or socks work well. Make it your individual signature, like I once experienced with Patrick the head of a big European luxury department store comparable with Bergdorf Goodman or Barneys in New York. Given his job, he was a very fashionable man who probably would have dressed in a style that was even more creative, eccentric, or exceptional. But given his job hierarchy and the dress code rules he had to follow in his responsible position, you didn't see him in anything other than a perfectly cut, custom-made, slim navy blue or charcoal suit, white crisp shirts, classy ties, and the most elegant pair of shoes. Only when the occasion allowed him to open or take off his jacket you were surprised by a splash of color— the loudest and brightest pink, yellow, purple or green inner lining with the most creative patterns. And here comes the highlight: He matched the color and pattern of the lining with those of his socks. Until today, I've no idea which tailor can make you matching socks for your jacket lining. But it shows perfectly that even in a very responsible leadership position that requires a traditional dress code, there is room for color and for individuality.

I don't want you to think colors themes don't matter at all. In fact, you should always take in consideration if the color flatters you, or not. Even if you want to show up in a spectacular color, if it's the worse color in your color themes you shouldn't choose it. However, traditional color consultants (or those who call themselves image consultants) often make you believe it's the only and most important decision to make. And I simply have to disagree, because you also have to bear in mind, if you'll be in the spotlight, if there are practical considerations, if the chosen colors express your individuality, or if there is a need for a symbolic message through the colors you wear.

🐦 Sylvie di Giusto @Sylvie_diGiusto
"What companies care about is consistency and professionalism
in their employees' appearance." #TheImageOfLeadership

Your Weight

When clients contact me because they feel uncomfortable with their weight, I honestly tell them that they must do two things that may seem to be contradictory.

1. You must accept your body as it is right now and have full confidence in yourself.
2. You must continually strive to improve your health and your fitness.

You must believe that at this very moment you have what it takes to succeed, and you must also be dedicated to making yourself better in every way.

You are perfect now. And you can, and should, strive to improve.

Contradictory ideas? Maybe.

Reality? Yes.

Do you think that you are overweight? Underweight? Maybe you are, maybe you aren't. Only you and your doctor can determine that. As long as you're healthy, that's all that matters. Do you need to alter your weight because your doctor told you to? Then don't wait. But you know that no matter what you may think about your weight, you need to succeed now. You are capable of being a leader now. If you're attending an important meeting or a job interview, you need to project a positive professional imprint. This begins with your attitude about yourself and is manifested in your personal ABCD: appearance, behavior, communication, and your digital footprint.

> 🐦 **Joel Thomas**
> **@joelericthomas**
> "Sometimes I think about being lazy. Then I remember how great winning is. I like winning."
> #TheImageOfLeadership

If you're overweight, have you chosen to change your eating habits and lose some excess pounds? Good! But do not say to yourself, "I'll be confident in a month, after I've lost ten pounds." That's a cop-out. There's no reason why you cannot have a powerful professional imprint today.

I cannot tell you how many wardrobes I've seen filled with clothes that were waiting for a supposedly upcoming weight loss. Some of those clothes hung there forever, some of them were even bought on purpose, thinking it would motivate their owner to lose weight. In fact, what should motivate my clients to lose weight is their health: high cholesterol, risk of heart disease, high blood pressure. Not that skinny skirt that does nothing else than take up space that could be used for well-fitting pieces, and demotivating my clients because they aren't losing the weight. You have a certain type of body right now. As a leader you want to feel and appear confident right now—not at some future date when those skinny clothes might fit you, right? Now! You need clothes that fit you right *now*.

🐦 **Meredeth McMahon**
@MeredethMcMahon

"Unless you plan to change your lifestyle through better diet & activity tomorrow, dress for the body you have today."
#TheImageOfLeadership

Here's a good example: New Jersey's Governor Chris Christie. It's undeniable that he's a very large man who has elevated himself to the national political stage. When you see the governor on television or at an event, it's impossible to ignore that he is struggling with obesity. (The late-night talk show hosts won't let anyone forget it, either!) For many voters, this could be a significant negative characteristic. A recent article from the *Wall Street Journal* showed that when it comes to leadership capabilities, the public at large sees overweight people as less qualified. This is a controversial and uncomfortable topic, but the truth is that you cannot ignore the studies done by the Center for Creative Leadership. Studies demonstrate that those with higher body-mass-index readings and larger waistlines are often perceived as less effective, in both interpersonal relations and performance.

Those are two important factors to consider for a man who stands on the national stage. Of course, the study does not suggest that people who carry excess weight are incapable of doing a good job. Governor Christie has proven himself a capable leader so far in New Jersey, all the more impressive when we consider that he is a Republican elected to office in a Democratic state.

Chris Christie does more than just act confidently. He also knows, or at least has been told, how to dress given his size. Anyone who knows how to dress well accentuates the positives while hiding the negatives as much as possible. And if a man fits into the category of big and tall—or, in the governor's case, *really* big and *averagely* tall—then he needs to be extra careful when it comes to his look. Big and tall men face some unique challenges when buying clothing, particularly dress clothes.

In terms of his business clothes Chris Christie thoroughly knows how to work around those challenges (or he's hired the right person to do so.) For instance, the first thing that you'll notice is the waistband of Governor Christie's suit trousers. Granted, it seems like a minor detail, but the majority of heavyset men insist on wearing their belt *underneath* their protruding stomach, at the narrowest point around their hips. Thus an overweight man can tell himself that he's wearing a belt that's "only" forty inches long, but this is only possible because he's wearing it down by his hips. But wearing the belt at the hips only further accentuates the bulge, which makes a person appear even more heavyset. It also wreaks havoc on the shirt, which is never long enough to cover the expanse of belly, and you see too many overweight men with their shirt buttons popping off and the shirttail coming out of the pants.

Chris Christie acknowledges his own weight and wears his pants correctly: they are belted *at the true waist.*

This is not something that matters exclusively to heavyset individuals, but goes for everyone who wears pants. You need to wear them in such a way to accentuate your form rather than having it focus on negatives.

With praise comes criticism, and in my opinion Christie's style is not always perfect. One adjustment that I would recommend could be his choice of the length of his neckties, which in his case is often far too long. Despite having a height of five-foot-eleven, Chris Christie makes himself look much shorter with the elongated ties that go against what a man of his build should be going for.

Christie's situation is reminiscent of America's most famously obese president, William Howard Taft. The twenty-seventh president stood five feet, eleven and a half inches tall—about the same as Chris Christie—and towards the end of his presidency in 1913 his weight peaked at 340 pounds. He was a very big man. Yet if you look at photos of Taft as an adult, you'll see that like Christie he's got his pants positioned at his natural waist, not on his hips. He also *always* wore traditional three-piece suits with a vest, fully buttoned. The vest usually matched the fabric of his dark suit and covered the waistband of his trousers. The vest was part of a continuously uniform fabric surface from his chest down to his legs, and created a slimming effect. When looking at a photo of Taft your eye has nothing to land on, and so your gaze is inexorably drawn up to his face, which is framed by a crisp white shirt and a silk necktie, and proudly crowned by his extravagant walrus moustache.

Every once in a while he wore a contrasting light-colored vest, but under the dark suit the effect was still slimming.

Speaking of obese chief executives, even four hundred and fifty years after his death just about everyone can visualize the infamous King Henry VIII of England. The full-length portrait by Hans Holbein the Younger is amazing in its audacity. The obese king, whose waist at its largest measured fifty-four inches, stands with legs apart, one hand on his hip, broad-shouldered, with every inch of his frame clothed in regal finery. He was the absolute monarch of all he surveyed, and he wanted you to know it. But when looking at the portrait, to what body part does your eye instantly gravitate? To the massive overfed belly? No! After being awed by the impossibly broad shoulders, what you see are the shapely legs, clad only in silk tights. The athletic, firmly rounded calves tapering to the slender ankles are worthy of a present-day pro football quarterback. They speak of youth and vitality, and tell you that no matter how immense the torso, this was a king who could stand on his own two feet.

🐦 **Summer Silvery @_sumerae**

"Just because you're skinny doesn't mean you're healthy."

#TheImageOfLeadership

The exceptions of King Henry VIII, President Taft, and Governor Christie notwithstanding, there are plenty of studies that suggest leaders are more successful when they appear to be fit and to have a healthy BMI. It appears to others that they have everything it takes to do their job competently. In addition to being perceived as ineffective, employers are concerned that overweight people will be sick more often, which will result in lost productivity and higher healthcare costs. Is it fair? Maybe not. But that's the way it is.

It's an unspoken prejudice. No client or employer will ever inform you that you didn't get the job, the promotion, or the contract just because you are overweight. However, don't forget your image is not what people actually tell you to your face; it's what they say and think behind your back. We think in stereotypes about overweight people. People's initial reaction to overweight leaders isn't positive.

As a leader, your physical aspects are quite important—maybe just as important as everything else. I just don't see a lot of obese Fortune 500 CEOs out there. While getting thinner doesn't directly impact that you'll become a Fortune 500 CEO, it shows that you are in control, that you are disciplined, and that you take care of yourself. It shows that this leader has the discipline and time management skills to exercise in the tiny amount of his or her free time. It shows that this leader takes care of himself or herself, and therefore people assume they can take care of others.

What doesn't work is if you use your weight as an excuse. Or if you complain about your body issues all the time but don't change anything. Or if you even make jokes about it.

Again, I'd like to mention Chris Christie as an example. On February 4, 2013 he appeared on *The Late Show* and told David Letterman he was the "healthiest fat guy you've ever seen." Letterman asked Christie how he felt about himself and the jokes they made about him, and Christie responded by pulling out a jelly donate and eating it during the interview. My opinion is that I've never seen him so inauthentic and insecure as in this scene. It just wasn't truthful, and wasn't the authentic Chris Christie many people knew. Later Christie went on the Don Imus radio show to announce that he would become "a big fat winner" in New Jersey and he joked about how much he weighed.

It had been an ongoing topic of discussion. In 2011 Christie revealed for the first time that he was trying to work out with a trainer in order to lose weight. Later in 2011 he told Piers Morgan on CNN that he felt guilty about his weight but didn't try to make excuses for it. It was also the year he got hospitalized for breathing problems and acknowledged that he would be healthier in general if he lost weight. The next year he said, "It's not as easy as you think, guys," and he compared obesity to taking drugs or drinking too much alcohol. He revealed that there are some people who are "incredible nasty, and ugly, and horrible, and prejudge him."

In December of 2012, Barbara Walters was one of the first people who asked him if he were too fat to become president, and he brushed off the question as being totally ridiculous. Shortly after that interview came the incident with the donut on the Letterman show. As he revealed in another interview later with Hilaria Baldwin, he said his plan is not being too sensitive with the comments about his weight, because you can't be "thin-skinned" about this stuff in his role. He also told reports about his dieting: "Sometimes I'm successful, and other times I'm not." (Not something you really want to hear from a leader, right?). When a former White House physician told CNN that if he were elected president there was a chance of him dying in office, he angrily responded, "She should shut up!"

In the end, we all know that in February 2013 he secretly underwent lap-band surgery.

The story I've just described shows Chris Christie occupying a space somewhere between jokes, guilt, anger, and ignorance.

So, making jokes, making excuses, making complaints about your weight is not the way to go. As a leader you've to show that you are very confident about the decisions you make about and for yourself, because only then will people trust you to have the ability to make tough decisions for others as well. What they see now in Christie is discipline, action, and the willingness to do what it takes to become a national leader. He makes people believe, that if he takes care of himself first, he'll be able to take care of many others. And he asks to be treated respectfully regardless his weight issues. I think it's a pretty smart decision.

> 🐦 **Megan Brandle**
> **@MegsImageGuide**
> "Take care of yourself first. Your self-worth impacts how others respond to you, and treat you."
> #TheImageOfLeadership

Aside from exceptions like Chris Christie as a society we tend to favor leaders who are not overweight. A recent research study co-authored by Mark Roehling, Michigan State University professor, and Patricia Roehling, professor of psychology at Hope College in Holland, Michigan, found that only five percent of male and female CEOs at top US companies had a body mass index (BMI) over thirty, which categorizes them as obese. This is much lower than the US average percentage of obese men and women, which as of this writing is 36 percent (men) and 38 percent (women) for the same age group.

However, evidence suggests that society places a double standard on the perception of excess weight on men and women. While obesity for anyone is not a good thing, obese men are given a "pass" more than women. The same study found that "between 45 percent and 61 percent of top male CEOs are overweight (BMI between 25 and 29)" but "only five percent to 22 percent of top female CEOs are overweight." Stated the researchers, "This reflects a greater tolerance and possibly even a preference for a larger size among men but a smaller size among women." As a society, physical appearance continues to play a role in workplace success, both in pay and promotions. Stated the Michigan study co-authors Mark Roehling

The Image of Leadership by Sylvie di Giusto

and Patricia Roehling, "It appears that the glass ceiling effect on women's advancement may reflect not only general negative stereotypes about the competencies of women, but also weight bias that results in the application of stricter appearance standards to women."

In addition, we have to mention the flip side of the coin: Those who are underweight. While I rarely have clients who are underweight, and there are no numbers and statistics out there if there is any influence in terms of being perceived as a leader, what I can attest to from my very own experience is that aside from fashion models, the image of underweight people is certainly not very different of overweight people. Everybody assumes that they are not healthy, that they don't take care of themselves, or that they have even profound issues like anorexia or bulimia. Society prejudges skinny people the same way that overweight people are prejudged. How can they possibly take care of others if they fail taking care of themselves?

> 🐦 Al Getler @AlGetler
> "Empty suit or well-rounded leader. Both have their wrinkles."
> #TheImageOfLeadership

A confident person works with the body he or she has. Confident people don't complain about their body issues. They take their body the way it is and work with it, or change it simply for the purpose of their own health. They seem to have no insecurities; instead they know how to stand out for the right reasons.

> 🐦 Sylvie di Giusto @Sylvie_diGiusto
> "Your image is not what people actually tell you to your face; it's what they say and think behind your back." #TheImageOfLeadership

Your Height

Why should height matter for a leader?

Consider the 2011 study entitled *The height leadership advantage in men and women: Testing evolutionary psychology predictions about the perceptions of tall leaders*, by a team led by Nancy M. Blaker from the VU University of Amsterdam (Netherlands) and the University of Oxford (UK). In their words: "Research suggests that tall individuals have an advantage over short individuals in terms of status, prestige, and leadership, though it is not clear why. Applying an evolutionary psychology perspective, we predict that taller individuals are seen as more leader-like because they are perceived as more dominant, healthy, and intelligent. Being fit and physically imposing were arguably important leadership qualities in ancestral human environments—perhaps especially for males—where being a leader entailed considerable physical risks. In line with our expectations, our results demonstrate that by manipulating an individual's stature height positively influences leadership perception for both men and women, though the effect is stronger for men. For male leaders this height leadership advantage is mediated by their perceived dominance, health, and intelligence; while for female leaders this effect is only mediated by perceived intelligence."

Here's how they performed the study. Two hundred and fifty-six participants were given pictures of business leaders to rate. Half of the participants saw a version of the leader in which he appeared to be short and the other half where the same leader appeared to be tall. Participants were asked to rate these individuals in terms of their leadership qualities. The majority of respondents rated the taller versions of the same person as more leader-like. The height leadership advantage was greater for men than for women leaders. Why did the participants prefer to be led by the taller choice? It had something to do with perceptions about their dominance and health. Our preference for taller leaders might be biologically hardwired, because in a dangerous ancestral environment, following a physically strong leader could have made the difference between life and death. The study's findings also showed that while taller women were perceived to be better leaders than shorter women, these same taller women were perceived as less leader-like when compared to shorter men. This had nothing to do with skill level, because taller female leaders were rated as more intelligent.

Are female leaders taller than average? Let's check the list of Fortune 500 CEOs and political leaders. Former Hewlett-Packard CEO and former California US Senate candidate Carly Fiorina is over five-foot seven inches tall. IMF Chief Christine Lagarde is six feet tall. German Prime Minister Angela Merkel is five-foot-five. President Cristina Fernandez de Kirchner of Argentina is five-foot-four. Former Prime Minister of Australia Julia Eileen Gillard stands five-foot-five.

So the results are mixed, at least for women. For men, a 2005 Fortune 500 survey found the average height of the US Fortune 500 CEO (a list mostly of men) is six-foot-two. But men of lesser stature need not despair; the tenth-richest man in America with a net worth of $31 billion and the former mayor of New York, Michael Bloomberg stands five-foot seven.

Consider Steve Ballmer, the former CEO of Microsoft. At six feet he is averagely tall, and he is stocky in build. For many the lasting impression of Ballmer is the sweaty, breathless, booming clown seen in countless Youtube clips, such as the "monkey boy" dancing from a decade ago. Ballmer has an enthusiasm that makes him appear to be even larger than he is. He is obviously not the best-dressed executive on the planet (although his look pretty much reflects his personality), but he effectively uses his height. You get the sense he could beat you up. He is very dominant, very powerful, and very impressive in his appearance. Just imagine if he were five feet tall—it would be a totally different experience to see him dancing like a monkey.

It also helps that Steve Ballmer is usually the only one on stage and not accompanied by others. As a leader, you want to make others as comfortable as possible. When you're tall, to do this you need to adjust your body language and be aware of your image. In my case, at five-foot-seven, I'm an average height. However, I usually wear high heels ranging from three to five inches, which gets me up to almost six feet. Many years ago I had the opportunity to present to the management board of a leading company a great concept for a group-wide training project. As a newcomer, it was a chance for me to present myself, my abilities, and my plans to this board, and I had to win their approval for a seven-figure budget. I only knew the management board members from anecdotes, from pictures on the intranet, and the monthly employee magazine. I entered the meeting room, properly dressed and wearing my best pair of power heels. I felt so confident. The board members were already seated. The presentation went very well and they approved my project and the budget.

To celebrate this major milestone, we called the communication department and asked them to take a quick photo of this important moment in the company's training and development strategy. When the board members stood up from their chairs around the meeting table, I was struck speechless. All of them were short—super short. I had no idea. The photographer positioned us next to each other in a row. When the magazine was published, no one talked about this major milestone, no one appreciated the accomplishment, and no one reached out to me to congratulate me for this quite important achievement during my early career. All I got was laughter and jokes about "The Daltons" picture—it's a well-known comic strip in Europe featuring one character who's excessively taller.

A friend to whom I told this story asked me if I had to do it over again, would I kick off my heels before the photo was snapped? No, I wouldn't. I think doing so would have made the others feel even more uncomfortable, and I wouldn't think it was very respectful. It might seem very condescending.

The answer is *preparation*. In today's digital world it takes me a few minutes to find out how people look, and there's a good reason everyone tells you to prepare this way for job interviews. Furthermore, I'm more aware of my height, and I use it efficiently. When I'm on stage alone, when I'm in front of a class, or when I'm doing a seminar I usually still wear my power high heels. Whenever I know that I've got to interact with people—such as in workshops, at consultations, or at a photo session—I'm very careful with my shoe choices.

Except for donning heels, you can't change your height; and as my personal example shows, by doing so I provoked a negative impression. I became much more aware of my choice of shoes and of my tall body. I try to avoid hovering and always sit down as soon as I possibly can, but I stand up straight when I've an important message to deliver. It's the entire package that counts.

I think it's important to understand it's not only about you. Earlier in the book I mentioned that Roger dressed well not out of vanity, but to make others feel confident and relaxed. The same is true for the examples of Mark Zuckerberg wearing a suit to meet the president of the United States, or Chris Christie wearing a fleece sweater while touring towns hit by Hurricane Sandy. It's important that you feel confident, but it's also important that you don't make others feel unconfident.

Another big challenge for tall people is that they cannot hide. Tall people are always public, and this can be pretty tough. Short people and those of average height can camouflage and sort of disappear in a crowd when they choose to—although many would argue that given a choice, most people who want to be leaders would choose to be taller than average.

The challenge with a perceived height issue is also that you can't change it in a long run. It's not like the weight issue, where you at least have the chance to lose or gain weight. There are some tools that image consultants can use to create optical illusions in order to help clients to make them appear taller. I can give every client the appearance of two to three inches additional in height, which is meaningful. All we do is we work with optical illusions. And you wouldn't think so, but people of short stature too often wear clothes that make them look even shorter. And the flip side is true too: tall people often choose clothes that make them even look taller. So they create optical illusions as well, they just use them the wrong way.

In terms of clothing, if you're not average or regular sized, whether you're a man or woman, you already know that you face the challenge that the retail industry has not a lot of options for you on the rack. For example, women who are between five-foot-five and five-foot-seven are thought of as "regular" sized. Everyone shorter is supposed to be "petite," everyone taller is supposed to be "tall." Although some brands and designers offer special collections for petite and tall people, the challenge is that the significant difference is their limbs, torso, rise and lower body. The height of some clients may be in their legs and not their torso, or vice-versa. The same is true with short people.

No fashion brand can accommodate all of those differences. Therefore, petite and tall women (and men) have to understand that for a perfect fit, you really need to consider custom-made clothes.

🐦 **Sylvie di Giusto @Sylvie_diGiusto**
"It's important that you feel confident, but it's also important that you don't make others feel unconfident." #TheImageOfLeadership

When You Need to Walk Down the Custom-Made Aisle

In this book I talk a lot about suits and business attire, and how necessary they are for any professional imprint. I also talk about how you need to work with the body you have.

If you're like most professionals, in the course of your career there will come a time when you should consider choosing custom-made clothing instead off pulling your business attire off the rack. Not only is it a visual sign that you give thought to your professional appearance, or that you're willing to invest in perfectly fitted and high quality pieces; it's simply a matter of fact that's related to your age. Our bodies naturally change as we age. Some of those changes cannot be avoided, although our lifestyle choices can either slow down this process or speed it up. After age thirty your muscles, body fat, weight, skin and even bones go through changes. Anyone reading this book who is over thirty knows what I'm talking about.

Your maturing body just isn't a standard body anymore. Unfortunately, off-the-rack clothes are made for standard bodies. Therefore, as soon as you are not the norm anymore, chances are remote that you'll find a perfectly fitting piece in a department store, boutique, or fashion outlet. Those who have always been "out of norm" because they are petite, plus size, or tall have to start this process even earlier.

When it comes to high-end business fashion for professionals, nothing beats custom-made clothes. Even though there is nothing inherently wrong with well-tailored clothes that people buy off the rack, it simply cannot compare to having clothes made to your specifications.

When you decide to buy custom-made clothing, you need to understand that there are two different ways to construct them:

1. Bespoke, and
2. Made-to-measure.

"Bespoke" is a British English word that means a clothing item made to a buyer's specifications. While the term historically is applied to only men's tailored clothing, it now generally includes footwear, fine jewelry and other apparel. The key points of bespoke tailoring are the buyer's total control over the fabric used, the features and fit, and the way the garment should be made. Bespoke describes a high degree of customization, and involvement of the end-user, in the production of the goods.

Bespoke clothing is cut from a pattern drafted from scratch for the customer. As a result, you have limitless options for the design of the suit because there is nothing to build on or adjust. This process differs from made-to-measure, produced to order from an adjusted block pattern, and from ready-to-wear or off-the-rack, which is factory made in finished condition and standardized sizes.

Over the last few years, the term "bespoke" has been hijacked by marketing and advertising gurus who were constantly pushing the boundaries of what type of effort would go into the production of a suit. Tailors very often use the term "bespoke" when it comes to custom-made clothes, because this has traditionally been considered the best way to create a personalized suit in accordance to the buyer's specification. There are even ads for bespoke suits you can order online, which is an absurd contradiction of terms.

It's important to know that bespoke has a very straightforward definition and you might spend a great deal of money assuming that your custom-made suit is going to be bespoke, which unfortunately is not always the case.

Nowadays, most of the tailors who advertise with bespoke are providing "made to measure," aka MTM. They still take measurements, still have a number of options to choose from, but the suit itself will be created based on an existing pattern. There is nothing inherently wrong with this, but you have to consider that this design process is not similar to true bespoke.

The options for women who look for custom-made clothes are very limited. They sometimes even don't have the choice to choose between bespoke or custom-made, and have to take whatever is available. Furthermore, most tailors are specialized menswear tailors, and only a few offer custom-made clothes for women too. I recommend my female clients to look for a tailor who does professional women's wear only. They are out there, even though there are not many yet. However, you always want to work with someone who is a specialist in his or her area, don't you?

Ultimately, no matter if you are a female or male leader, you need to determine for yourself what your requirements are. If you're willing to invest the money and are able to wait for your suit, there is nothing better than a bespoke suit. If you're going to get a MTM suit, it's a great choice as well.

If you cannot afford bespoke, it's not the end of the world. The president of the United States does very well in suits that are made-to-measure by HartMarx (formerly Hart, Schaffner & Marx), the venerable Chicago-based company founded in 1887. The Obama suit, as it is now called, is always the same style and material—a two-button, single-breasted suit jacket and single pleated pant with inch-and-a-quarter cuffs, and is made of a ninety-seven percent worsted wool and three percent cashmere blend.

As Forbes reported in August 2008, just before Barack Obama accepted the Democratic nomination, the Obama suit has a flattering fit and a soft drape, and the material has a nice feel against the skin. Lisa Wells, director of public relations for Hickey Freeman, a subsidiary of HartMarx, said, "The silhouette is a classic fit; he's a forty long with a thirty-three-inch waist." Cynthia O'Connor, founder and CEO of Cynthia O'Connor + Company, a women's fashion and accessories showroom in New York City and Los Angeles, said it was a good choice. "This suit is tailored, contemporary and an Italian cut, which tends to fit closer to the body. It is not the traditional conservative suit. If you put it next to Senator John McCain's suit, McCain immediately looks ten years older.... What's interesting is Obama is really portraying a different image than what the other candidates have displayed. He is appealing to a younger audience in both how he looks and dresses. He is on trend, which is all part of his package and appeal." According to Forbes, a comparable suit would sell off the rack for $1,500 at department stores such as Nordstrom.

No matter your height or size, custom-made or off-the-rack clothes, the most important thing is that you "own" your body. That you know the impression it leaves behind in terms of your leadership skills. Are you the big impressive bear (as I would describe Steve Ballmer) who knocks everyone down who's in his way? Are you slender like Condoleezza Rice, or a substantial woman like Oprah Winfrey? Whatever you are, don't apologize! You are who you are, and you have to work with what you have. Make the best out of it. Present yourself in the best possible version of yourself.

🐦 Sylvie di Giusto @Sylvie_diGiusto

"Whatever you are, don't apologize! You are who you are,
and you have to work with what you have." #TheImageOfLeadership

Leaders Are Confident About Their Age

I recently helped a lovely realtor named Mary Ann. She's a wonderful woman who has been successful in her profession for a long time. However, she had to step back for a few years because of some personal medical challenges she was facing, and also because she had to take care of her sick mother at home. When she was able to return to the workforce she had just turned fifty-six, and she hired me for a personal consultation. She told me she was scared to compete against all those young women applying for the same jobs. She asked me to help her in order to make her appear much younger.

Honestly, her challenge was not that she wanted to look younger. Her challenge was that life has beaten this wonderful woman down and she didn't even look like fifty-six, which is hardly over the hill. She just looked tired—very, very tired. She had forgotten about herself and made herself look so much older. If you saw her on the street, you'd probably guess she was close to seventy.

It was an easy game to bring her back on track. And, no, afterwards she didn't look like she was thirty-five; she looked like fifty-six, exactly her age. She looked like a successful, happy, and confident fifty-six-year-old woman. She looked age-appropriate.

I don't think that age-appropriate is defined by any number. I've met many women in their 50s who are in amazing shape and can pretty much pull off any outfit. What's age-appropriate for one leader can be very different for another. The key to appearing age-appropriate is paying attention to what feels right on you.

Yes, a professional image consultant can give you a few years up and down in your appearance. So can a makeup artist, a hairdresser, and—no question at all—a plastic surgeon. But, in terms of confidence and age-appropriate appearance, we can all learn a lesson from the nonagenarian style icon Iris Apfel, who said, "I believe it was Chanel who said, 'Nothing makes a woman look so old as trying desperately hard to look young.' You can look smashing at any age, especially if you have good posture. Never try to compete with younger co-workers by wearing short skirts, ruffles and tight sweaters."

Success can come at any age. "Colonel" Harlan Sanders was sixty-five when he began touring the country and selling Kentucky Fried Chicken franchises. Mary Kay Ash retired from a nondescript corporate job at age of forty-five before founding Mary Kay Cosmetics, which made her a multi-millionaire. Tim and Nina Zagat, the couple behind the Zagat dining surveys, were each forty-two years when they started their business. Ronald Reagan might have been a famous actor before, but was fifty-five years old when he got elected to his first public office. And who knows, we might have a seventy-year-old president ahead, when Hillary Clinton will presumably run. On the other end of the age spectrum, there are plenty of examples of young entrepreneurs becoming successful leaders and business owners. No matter if young or old, they all have something in common: they look age-appropriate; exactly the way people expect them to look at their age.

Consider the story of "The Young Aristocrat". This was a nickname given to Joe, a very ambitious and talented young man by his co-workers, his supervisor, his team members, his training manager—and even from me! He had an eloquent surname, and indeed he looked like those fortunate aristocrats who live a careless and perpetually youthful life. No matter how old he became, Joe always looked like he was twenty-one. He seemed to have found the mythical Fountain of Youth.

While women dream of endless youthfulness, men can find it to be a handicap. As long as I watched his career path, Joe never got a position that matched the amazing skills he brought to the table. Why not? Perhaps it was his choice of wardrobe. He made an effort to dress himself very traditionally in order to look much older, but he actually went too far. He tried too hard.

While his suits were quite expensive and of great quality, he chose very traditional fabrics, very traditional cuts, and a very traditional overall look. Such wardrobe choices are great for corporate America, for politicians, and anyone who needs a very traditional image. But ironically, with such a look even a young man can easily look old-fashioned. Joe looked like a teenager dressed in his grandpa's clothes! Just imagine a dashing twenty-five-year-old man you know wearing Roger Moore's suits. There's nothing wrong with Roger Moore's suits. They're just not made for a dynamic young leader. They're made for mature men like Roger Moore.

Joe always was, and always will be, "The Young Aristocrat." Eventually, he left the corporate world in the meantime.

While on the subject of age and attitudes towards age, let's dive into the saga of Mike Jeffries, the CEO of clothing retailer Abercrombie & Fitch. Besides the controversial statements he has made, I've found it quite interesting that his press coverage is often accompanied by commentary about his personal appearance. The numerous plastic surgeries he has obviously had in order to look younger have become a lively topic of discussion in the general public.

Sites such as Reddit, Digg, and the Twitter community have been quick to lampoon Jeffries for his personal style. At age sixty-nine, it is understandable that the CEO would show signs of aging. However, unlike many other older men who decide to age gracefully, Jeffries has evidently undergone numerous plastic surgery procedures. From the look of it, he has had lip injections, a possible nose job, a browlift, and a facelift. When you see a man who can legally retire dressed like a kid in flip-flops and Abercrombie polo shirts and sweaters, it sets him up for ridicule. He's the CEO of a multimillion-dollar company, and while it is true that his relaxed style has garnered him some attention in the past, at some point it's important to look and dress your age. While recent appearances have seen him dress in a more conservative way, there is no doubt the man's own sense of style leaves a lot to be desired. Quite interesting for the head of a supposedly exclusive fashion retailer.

While some of the comments made towards Mike Jeffries have been incredibly mean spirited, one cannot help but wonder whether this is something that was inevitable. If you build a brand out of being exclusionary and only want to hire the most beautiful young models to work with you, chances are that people are going to hold you to those same standards.

> **Shanna Wu Pecoraro**
> **@SPImage**
> "Aging starts from the mind not the body. We all grow more beautiful when wisdom is on our side."
> #TheImageOfLeadership

And if you're looking for an opposing example, consider American fashion designer and business executive Ralph Lauren. His Ralph Lauren brands are a global multi-billion-dollar enterprise with 2013 sales of $6.92 billion, giving the company a Forbes ranking of #86 in the world's most valuable brands. At age seventy-five, he looks his age and looks terrific. He's always photographed in upscale settings, immaculately attired in either casual or business dress, and looking every inch a member of the landed gentry. As of September 2012, Forbes estimated his wealth at $6.5 billion dollars, which made Ralph Lauren the 162nd richest person in the world.

Yes, there are those great tips and tricks an image consultant can give you; and indeed we sometimes work wonders by just letting a man grow a beard to look more experienced or older. But in the end, you've to be aware of your age. Confident leaders don't dress themselves fundamentally younger, and they don't dress themselves significant older. Dress according to your age, and show what you're able to deliver.

> **Sylvie di Giusto @Sylvie_diGiusto**
> "Confident leaders don't dress themselves fundamentally younger, and they don't dress themselves significant older." #TheImageOfLeadership

Leaders Are Confident About Their Gender

Women sometimes propose to me the idea that they should dress more like a man in order to be more accepted in their male-dominated working environments. In training sessions I make fun of that idea by walking over to the first man I find in the room. I ask him with an ironic undertone, "James, we think you appear a little bit too dominant, a little bit too bossy, a little bit too macho, a little bit too masculine. Would you mind dressing a little bit more like a woman, a little bit more feminine?" Everyone agrees that this would be a crazy suggestion. I think that women should not try to hide behind their masculine suits, using them as a protective shield against the rough-and-tough man's world. They adopt them to feel more equal with them, to be "one of them." They hope to be perceived as more serious, more dominant, more eye-to-eye, and on the same level. However, I really disagree with this, because I think women should not sacrifice their femininity. Men wouldn't sacrifice their masculinity, would they?

A recent article in the UK *Telegraph* revealed that one in four women dress in a more masculine way—such as exchanging high heels and dresses for pantsuits—under the belief that to be treated seriously they should look like their male colleagues. The survey of two thousand working women showed that another quarter wear less makeup at work, partly to dispel the notion that all women must "look pretty."

Half hide their true emotions, with two fifths admitting to having left the office to cry. A fifth believe they need to act ruthlessly to be respected at work. A small number, one in twenty, actively mirror the behavior of male colleagues.

Why do so many women feel the need to look or act like their male colleagues in order to succeed? A research, by telecommunications firm O2, suggested the lack of female role models at the top of business was partly to blame. One in ten women said there are no females in senior positions at their company, while forty-two percent said senior women act like alpha females to get ahead, which leads many women to assume more traditionally "male" characteristics in order to be successful.

Ann Pickering, O2's UK human resources director, said, "While businesses today have come a long way from the offices of *Mad Men*, the reality is that many modern women are still feeling the pressure to conform to outdated stereotypes... Having a truly diverse workforce—one in which all employees are encouraged to act and behave as themselves—is not just about what is proper and fair, it also makes complete business sense."

Dress for the gender you have, and for nothing else. I recommend that women acknowledge their female body features, to show that they are women. You've just got to be careful not too show too much! Of course the same is true for men, who may need to observe the fine line of not over-exaggerating their masculinity.

No discussion of gender-appropriate dress would be complete without mentioning Hillary Clinton and her famous pantsuits. A variation on the standard men's suit with a blazer and slacks, the pantsuit was first introduced in the 1920s, when a small number of women adopted a masculine style, including pantsuits, hats, and even canes and monocles. Film star Katharine Hepburn often wore slacks, and said, "Skirts are hopeless. Anytime I hear a man say he prefers a woman in a skirt, I say, 'Try one. Try a skirt.'" Hepburn cultivated her counter-culture image deliberately, eventually ordering custom-made slacks and shoes. "I think you should pretend you don't care," she once remarked to Greta Garbo, who had captivated Hollywood with her mannish suits, hats, and Ferragamo flat-heeled shoes. "But it's the most outrageous pretense. I bet it takes us longer to look as if we hadn't made any effort than it does someone else to come in beautifully dressed.'"

André Courrèges introduced long trousers for women as a fashion item in the late 1960s, and over the next forty years pantsuits gradually became acceptable business wear for women. Nonetheless, pantsuits were often deprecated as inappropriately masculine clothing for women, and many in-stitutions resisted. For example, until the 1990s, women were not permitted to wear pantsuits in the United States Senate. The House of Representa-tives was slightly more permissive; according to the *Washington Post*, in December 1969 Congresswoman Charlotte T. Reid showed up on the last day before recess "in a black wool, bell-bottomed pantsuit... a first in the annals of the US Congress." Many male colleagues ran to the floor to gawk, she told The Post, but all were kind. "Gerald Ford [then the minority leader] told me he thought it was great, and I should do it more often."

Proponents of the pantsuit cite advantages including comfort, modesty, and the reduced need for pantyhose. Hillary Clinton became an enthusiastic adopter of pantsuits, and referred to her 2008 presidential campaign staff as "The Sisterhood of the Traveling Pantsuits." Her signature style, tailored in the Beverly Hills atelier of her longtime suit designer Susanna Chung Forest, keeps her looking like a leader even under pressure. With tailored pants and longer jackets that are nipped in at the waist and skim the hip, Clinton shows that business dressing for women can be attractive, age-appropriate, comfortable, and wrinkle-free, even while traveling around the globe.

Another great designer who masters this art is Alvin Valley. *The New York Times* has called him "The King of Pants"—and rightly so! Best known for the fantastic fit of his long-legged pants, Valley has quickly become a force in the New York fashion community. Born in New York but raised in Spain, after graduating from the University of Miami, he opened his first boutique in Coconut Grove, Florida in 1995. Valley has developed a loyal clientele of socialites and celebrities, as well as a retail distribution network spanning the US, Japan, and China.

He understands a woman's body and he understands construction. Using high-end fabrics and techniques which are often used in menswear tailoring, he designs the most beautiful and modern pants on a high fashion point, which can be worn and dressed up or down from party night to corporate office.

Valley once said in an interview, "Culturally, when you grow up around Latinas, you understand a different point of view of women and power. No matter what, you can still be sexy while powerful, and that's innate in the cut and silhouette of these pants.... When clients put on my pants they feel empowered. I don't feel they should look less attractive when they're in the workplace with men."

The *New York Times* calls him the King. I say, once in her lifetime every woman should experience a pair of pants from the "King of Pants".

Many of Alvin Valley's clients, or Hillary Clinton are perfect examples of not pushing it too hard and making wardrobe choices that over-exaggerate femininity by showing every part of the body to prove it is a woman. Instead, they choose pieces, which might originate from a masculine wardrobe and make them look feminine, professional, and particularly age-appropriate.

🐦 **Sylvie di Giusto @Sylvie_diGiusto**
"Women should not hide behind their masculine suits as a protective shield against the rough-and-tough man's world." #TheImageOfLeadership

The Rules Don't Change

The same rules apply if we dress a body that is not the gender the person wants to have. I currently work with a client named Theresa who self-identifies as a woman but has lived more than forty years in the body of a man. She now is transitioning to a life, both personal and professional, as a woman. When I first met Theresa, her major challenge was that she didn't dress gender-appropriately as a woman. Not one professional woman would have had those clothes in her wardrobe that she insisted upon wearing, "just to show that I'm a woman now." I once told her, "You look like a corporate drag queen." We both had a good laugh and she agreed that she had gone too far.

As a leader or someone who wants to be a leader, don't let your gender become a topic in any way. This is true for women, for men, for gay, for straight, for transgenders. In addition, don't let your sexual choices become a topic. You'll recall Jasper, my colorful and bright client with his lemon yellow shirt, grass green pants, orange loafers—"everybody's darling, always on the bright side of life." Yes, he was gay, and he frankly celebrated the flamboyant stereotype in his fashion style, in his body language, and in his communication. He even mentioned it on his LinkedIn profile. But think about it—what specific skill would a man or woman bring to the corporate world that related to being gay, or straight? Unless you wanted to work for a specifically gay interest group or gay publication, why would you mention it on your LinkedIn profile? Does it make him a better corporate lawyer? Would any recruiter contact him on LinkedIn just because he mentioned his sexual orientation?

Anyway, who cares? It's the twenty-first century! You want to be hired and promoted because of your skills and your experience, right?

In advanced industrialized countries, sexual orientation is becoming less of an issue. In the US Congress, Representative Barney Frank can claim the distinction of being the first gay man to serve openly—he came out in 1987. Senator Tammy Baldwin became the first openly gay US Senator when she was elected in 2012. David Nicola Cicilline has been the US representative for Rhode Island's First Congressional District since 2011. From 2003 to 2011 he served as mayor of Providence, Rhode Island, and was the first openly gay mayor of a US state capital. In 2012, Major General Patricia

"Trish" Rose became the first openly lesbian two-star general in the US Air Force, and the highest ranking openly gay officer in the entire US military at the time.

Jóhanna Sigurðardóttir, elected the prime minister of Iceland in 2009, became the first openly gay head of government in modern times. Xavier Bettel is Luxembourg's first gay prime minister. Nikki Sinclaire is the U.K.'s first openly transgender parliamentarian.

Theresa Sparks, who is a transgender, is the executive director of the San Francisco Human Rights Commission and was a candidate for San Francisco supervisor for District 6 in the November 2010 election. Regarding her transformation from male to female, she told the *San Francisco Chronicle*, "It's an unusual condition, but it's not unnatural. You discover that the only way to live with it is to transition physically so your physical appearance matches how you feel about yourself." In the corporate world there's Tim Cook, CEO of Apple, or Anderson Cooper, anchor of CNN news and the most prominent openly gay journalist on American TV. No one really cares that they are gay. It's not a topic; they don't dress, talk, or behave in any way that's different than any other person or leader.

The point of all of this is to reiterate the ironclad concept that *you dress to make yourself look your very best in every situation*. Period.

In the end, no matter what specifics your body has in terms of weight, height, age, gender, or sexuality, I want you to be confident about it. Without confidence, there is no leadership. Because, people don't listen to those who are unsure of themselves.

I'm inspired by the story of former New York Governor David Paterson, who got an infection at age three that left him almost totally blind. His disability did not stop him from believing that he could be a leader. A 1983 graduate of Hofstra Law School, he was elected to the New York State Senate in 1985. Less than twenty years later, he had risen to the position of senate minority leader. Eliot Spitzer, former Governor of New York, selected Paterson as his running mate in the 2006 New York gubernatorial election, and Paterson took office as lieutenant governor on January 1, 2007. When Spitzer resigned in the wake of a prostitution scandal, Paterson was sworn in as governor of New York on March 17, 2008. He served until 2010. When asked by the *New York Daily News* about his disability, Paterson said, "Only in the last few years of my life did I become comfortable having people see me publicly display that I have a disability.... Now to be able to be myself and publicly have it known...I think there's a lot of people who have a lot of different problems who feel more empowered from that. If that's the case, then I'm feeling pretty good about that aspect of the job."

There are many more stories about individuals who have overcome stereotypes and any kind of challenges, to assume positions of leadership. If you want something badly enough, you'll do what it takes to get there!

🐦 **Sylvie di Giusto @Sylvie_diGiusto**
"If you want something badly enough, you'll do what it takes to get there!"
#TheImageOfLeadership

Chapter 4
Leaders Look
Authentic

 Marc Jacobs @marcjacobs
"To me, clothing is a form of self-expression – there are hints about who you are in what you wear." #TheImageOfLeadership

I n terms of choosing your clothes and defining your appearance, one of the best attitudes you can take is to say, "What you see is what you get!" Nothing is worse than someone who is trying to be something they're not. The harder they try, the more they come off as inauthentic and phony.

People are usually surprised when I tell them that New Jersey's Governor Chris Christie is one of the best-dressed leaders in this country. In the years ahead I think this will remain true whether he stays at his current weight or becomes more slender; but as of this writing, he's a very large man. He has to dress one heck of a body, and he always does it very well in terms of cut, fabric, and fit of his suits. But he's also very authentic in what he does, what he says, and how he looks. Everything about him says, "That's what you get. Nothing else. That's me."

Leaders often say things to please others and to look good in front of the crowd. Not "Jersey Boy" Christie. He consistently talks "truth". It doesn't come from his title or from his size or from his paycheck. Instead, this form of leadership simply comes from the being and the person he truly is: "Jersey Boy" Christie.

Consider his fleece jacket, which became a signature part of his look in the aftermath of Hurricane Sandy. It was the right look for the moment: practical, subdued, workmanlike. It said, "I'm in charge, but I'm one of you. We're all in the same boat right now." It's a simple wardrobe piece that helps him deliver this important message.

As another example, let's return to Miley Cyrus. She left behind the cute Hannah Montana image and has demonstrated what she wants to be as a grown-up entertainer. She doesn't try to be another version of Hannah Montana, she doesn't try to be a copy of Madonna, and she doesn't try to be Taylor Swift either. She is consistent and clear about the image she wants us to create in our minds when we think about her. One of her main instruments to do this is the choice of her clothes. Her wardrobe items are not made by accident, nor are they driven by fashion trends or personal style preferences. They are intentionally chosen to demonstrate the new image. You just have to look at her and everyone knows who she is.

Like it or not, people also have expectations that you can either fulfill or defy. Ninety-nine percent of the time, you will want to fulfill people's expectations of who you are based on your appearance. For example, in my training sessions I usually show my audience seven pictures of men and women, each wearing some variation of a two-piece suit. I ask my audience which of those they would hire as their divorce lawyer, which one would they trust as their plastic surgeon, which one would they expect on a stage as a professional speaker, which one would they like to see as their children's school principal. Almost invariably, the answers and choices are always the same.

Those very few individuals who defy expectation—the flamboyant lawyer, for example, who dresses in snakeskin cowboy boots and sports a rhinestone jacket—are few and far between. If you are inclined to emulate someone like that, you're already doing it, and you're not reading this book.

As the concept of confirmation bias has proven, people connect certain characteristics with a person's physical appearance. The way you look on the outside sends subtle cues about what you could be like on the inside, and which characteristics you bring to the table. Simply said, do you look like someone who is trustworthy? Or creative? Or dominating? Or approachable? Within the first seven seconds of meeting you, the person will be inclined to believe that you have those qualities.

🐦 Sylvie di Giusto @Sylvie_diGiusto
"Don't try to be something you're not. The harder you try, the more you come off as inauthentic." #TheImageOfLeadership

Keywords Are the Keys to Authenticity

We all have certain pictures of those people in our heads, and while they may not all look the same, they have a lot in common. The divorce lawyer we are looking for will always wear a very traditional suit, maybe navy blue or charcoal with a modest white shirt and, for men, a conservative tie. We want him or her to look this way because their clothes obviously send the message that they are reliable, authoritative, trustworthy, and consistent.

Is there anything exceptional or remarkable about this outfit? No, there isn't. Is there anything extraordinarily creative about this outfit? No, there isn't either, but we also do not expect it, and it's not expected by the legal profession either. The keyword we associate with the legal profession is "trust," not "creativity."

The two-piece suit we see worn by a creative head of marketing in a multi-media firm or the head of the buying department in a retail company looks very different, but it's still a suit. It might have an extraordinary fabric with an eccentric pattern and unique style details, combined with a colorful shirt, and may be worn with a bright bowtie or some accessories that are out of the ordinary. The keyword in marketing is "creativity" not "trust."

> 🐦 **Maria Schwartz Esq.**
> **@Divorcemuse**
> "How I look is how they will feel, is what I always tell myself when dressing for court."
> #TheImageOfLeadership

There are certain style personalities who work very well for certain industries and professions. The most authentic leaders in the world are consistent in what they wear every day. Some are known for their elegant aesthetic, others for their creative appearance. No matter which signature look they have chosen, it consistently says something about them and the person they are—and about the keyword they have chosen.

For example, English businesswoman, fashion designer, model and singer Victoria Beckham chooses each of her wardrobe pieces and the great runway looks she designs with the utmost elegance and drama. Her keyword

> 🐦 **Jessica Kupferman**
> **@JessKupferman**
> "Consistency is the #1 key to a successful personal brand. You can't create a good brand with 7 different fonts."
> #TheImageOfLeadership

as a fashion designer is "drama." And indeed, while she comes across as someone who is reserved, stands above such things like criticism, has everything under control, and is in charge—everything is stage-managed to appear "dramatic". Although she had quite an interesting life story on her own so far, you'd probably not want to hire her as your life coach, would you? Because the keyword for life coaches is not "drama" but "receptiveness," and we want those people to be, act, and look approachable.

A common method that image consultants use to help clients identify their keywords and to adjust their appearance based on those keywords and the given job requirements are style personalities. There are seven of them, at least in the system I use that was developed by Alyce Parsons in her book *StyleSource: The Power of the Seven Universal Styles for Women and Men.*

1. Traditional (keyword: e.g. trust)
2. Elegant (keyword: e.g. quality)
3. Creative (keyword: e.g. extraordinariness)
4. Romantic (keyword: e.g. receptiveness)
5. Dramatic (keyword: e.g. power)
6. Alluring (keyword: e.g. glamour)
7. Natural (keyword: e.g. comfort)

Each piece in your wardrobe can be assigned to a certain style personality. For example, a woman who wears a pastel colored, soft, unstructured, flowing blouse with ruffles, paired with a cute A-line skirt and a fitted jacket in cream would be considered to be a "romantic" style personality. Supportive, caring, warm and nurturing are the attributes we automatically link to this person. Therefore, this style personality works especially well in professions that are people-related, such as counseling, social working, teaching, or nonprofit.

🐦 **Meredeth McMahon**
@MeredethMcMahon

"List adjectives you want people to use to describe you. Those must guide your professional image."
#TheImageOfLeadership

If you dress traditionally—meaning a navy blue two-piece-suit, with white shirt, silk tie, and black oxford shoes for a man—you're presenting an image that appears reliable, authoritative, trustworthy, and consistent. If you believe those are important traits for your job (such as management positions or financial consulting) then dress like this. If you're working in a creative position (marketing or advertising), chances are these are not necessarily the first characteristics that managers and colleagues are looking for.

Each person combines up to three of those style personalities and reflects them in their wardrobe.

What if the style personality you adore doesn't match the keyword that is necessary for your industry or profession? Can you just fake it? Certainly not.

You cannot jump into a creative style personality if you're not a creative person and there's not one creative piece in your wardrobe. People who try this are those who look inauthentic. You see them on the street or in the office and instantly you think, "Something is wrong here." However, you can accentuate and emphasize certain style personalities and use the characteristics that are connected to them. You can increase one style personality more than the other, for example in your private life compared to your professional one. You can borrow elements from other style personalities as well. But don't "dress up," because the opposite happens: You appear inauthentic.

🐦 **Dean Deguara**
@Deandeguara
"Authenticity is acknowledging the best version of me is the real me."
#TheImageOfLeadership

This is where an image consultant certainly can help you. It's not about boxing you into a particular style. Instead you might need help with analyzing your own style personality, determining the best style personality for your industry and profession, and filling the gap. In addition, working with a consultant can boost your fashion confidence and reduce time and money you spend shopping.

Because here is another secret: Fashion designer, tailors, and brands work as well into these style personalities. If you are just a little bit like the way Victoria Beckham is or dresses, or if you have an eye for Daniel Craig's sleek suits in the James Bond films, you are certainly someone who is within the style personality "dramatic." You'd die for a piece of Tom Ford and could certainly shop every item at Chanel. However, if you go to Burberry it feels somehow strange to you. You'll probably find that one piece that comes closest to your style personality, but after being worn one or two times it will live a long and lonesome life in your wardrobe... hanging around.

🐦 Sylvie di Giusto @Sylvie_diGiusto
"The most authentic leaders in the world are consistent in what they wear every day."
#TheImageOfLeadership

Being Liked Is Not the Goal

I have female clients who tell me that no one sees them as powerful, strong women; instead everyone thinks that they're cute and nice. And then they stand in front of me with their cute curls, in a cute ponytail with a cute scrunchie, with their cute apricot make up and a cute lip gloss, decorated with cute jewelry, wearing a cute polka dot pastel blouse with cute ruffles, and a cute flowery flower skirt with cute little shoes with a cute little bow on them. And I say: "Well, maybe it's because cuteness is oozing from every pore of your body!" I promise you, they sit in their cute offices with cute decorations on their office desk, cute holiday cards and cute family pictures all over, and a cute bowl of sweet candies to offer to their cute guests. Everything about them is cute.

The type of woman I just described is within a style personality that I call "romantic." The message they are sending is this: "Please like me." Now let's think about this. In business, is it important to be liked? It's a subtle concept, but the answer is "no." In business, you need to work well with other people. You need to be polite. You need to have respect for others and be respected. You need to have leadership qualities. But at the end of the day, seeking the personal affection of your colleagues—both above you and below you on the ladder—is irrelevant.

Remember the story about the leadership training with horses, and those who entered the horse arena with the strategy of wanting to be liked by the horse? Are you aware of whether anyone "liked" Abraham Lincoln? Henry Ford? How about Bill Gates, Janet Yellen, Carly Fiorina? Their personal friends and family members like them, but in the business world it's not part of the equation.

As they say in the rough political world of Washington, D.C., "If you want a friend, get a dog." That's a bit extreme (except in Washington), but the point is that your job as a leader is to earn respect. Being liked is far down on the list.

But how do we shape the romantic individual into a leader? Would it work if we just convinced the romantic client to wear a few very traditional or dramatic pieces? No, because she wouldn't feel comfortable and she wouldn't appear authentic. Authenticity is one of the few things that you simply can't fake it 'til you make it. It would be like the wrong person in the wrong clothes. Instead, I teach these wonderful women to borrow elements from other style personalities to look more powerful, more traditional, stronger, and to skip some of their romantic elements that make them appear relentlessly cute. Those women have to identify those elements that label them as "cute." It

The Image of Leadership by Sylvie di Giusto

could be the flowery skirt, as well as their office desk, their humble body language, or their squeaky voice. Honestly, in most cases we have a little bit of everything.

Lest you think I'm trying to wring all of the humanity out of you, the opposite is true too. People sometimes tell me that others think they are not approachable and that they can't connect with others. Guess what? No cuteness here; in nine out of ten cases, their entire wardrobe is black, and excessively dramatic. My clients tell me that others think they are not innovative, but boring; sure enough, most of their wardrobes are grey. Others face the challenge that they are overlooked all the time. In most cases their wardrobes are beige. And beige, brown, green are important colors for those who I group into the style personality of "natural." A style where comfort is king, but shopping for an office outfit is just evil for them.

What you wear sends signals to other people. I know this may sound weird, but those style personalities and the related keywords can indeed be the key to your success. They show you who you are as a person, and how others perceive you. I can break them down from the colors you have in your wardrobe, the cut of your clothes, the accessories you choose, the nail polish on your fingers, the way you style your hair, the car you drive, the food you eat, the type of vacation you book, and even the personality of the husband or wife you marry.

What you wear says something about who you are. Your clothes speak very loudly!

🐦 Sylvie di Giusto @Sylvie_diGiusto

"What you wear says something about who you are. Your clothes speak very loudly! "
#TheImageOfLeadership

The Natural Personality vs. The Professional

Let's again mention Mary Ann, the real estate agent who wanted to look younger. The years she was out of the workforce were challenging because of a personal health issue in addition to her responsibilities taking care of her sick mother. She spent a lot of time at home, day after day after day. Of course this had an influence on the way she dressed, on the way she took care of herself, and on the way she was perceived by others. The way she described herself, and the feedback she got from others, was that basically she became "comfortable". And that was it: Every piece she bought for her wardrobe during the last years was designated to the fact that it had to be comfortable. The fabrics she chose were comfortable, the cuts she chose were comfortable, even the colors she chose screamed "comfortable." Her keyword was "comfort."

The keyword "comfort" is represented by a style personality I call "natural." There are two kinds of people who embody this style personality.

First are the ones who choose this style on purpose because they identify with everything about it and it's part of their entire lifestyle. For example, in addition to their khaki cargo pants, they probably drive a Jeep Wrangler, go on Safari to Africa, and would always choose a campfire outside instead of a fancy night at a club. They choose to be this way and therefore they look this way. They are absolutely authentic and I wouldn't change a thing.

This is not Mary Ann.

Second are those who just slipped into it because their lifestyle changed. For example, these might be the moms who have to stay at home after having children and people who have become work-at-home entrepreneurs. They have no particular reason to "dress up," and so they wear whatever's comfortable. These are also people who have the wherewithal and circumstances that allow a low-maintenance and comfortable life.

Can you see Mary Ann within this group?

For the first group, it would be no challenge to find an office outfit, even with a natural style personality. Those people just can "rock" that style, wherever, at home or in the office. And indeed there are many professions where this style personality works really well, such as information technology, and software development, or teaching.

For the second group who accidently slipped into the natural personality, it can be tough. Because the truth is that a) it's not really her or him, b) they try to make it somehow work, and c) it's not the right style personality for the industry or profession they are in.

Yes, Mary Ann was at home, and she had to take care of herself and of others, but "comfortable" is just not the primary characteristic we want to see in a real estate agent, is it? The natural style personality is simply wrong for Mary Ann.

What we want to see is someone who takes care of the money we entrust to him or her in the best possible way. We're looking for energy, attention to detail, and professional toughness. The least important thing we want to see is that he or she is comfortable. The keyword for real estate agents instead is "responsibility." Therefore, Mary Ann had to learn to borrow elements from the elegant style personality.

Each of the seven style personalities works very well within the appropriate industry. It's because every career path has some kind of uniform that signals that you belong in this position or to this industry. This uniform might vary widely, but it exists. Creative industries (media, fashion, public relations, advertising, publishing) have always allowed employees to dress a bit more informally and stylishly. This tells clients that they are creative, daring, willing to test limits, and not look like everyone else. This is what clients expect and want from creative people. An investment banker instead has only a narrow range of conservative choices, and everything about him or her has to verify that the client's choice is safe, it's stable, it's fine—exactly like their investments. Likewise with attorneys; the keyword for them is "trust." For social workers it's "approachable," and for HR managers it's "responsible." We expect people in high-tech to look a little bit "nerdy" right? Which is just a not very nice way to say they are very intelligent. They're not concerned with looking cool because they're too busy thinking of amazing things.

Mary Ann spent years in her comfort zone at home where she could wear her comfortable clothes. She needed to take a fresh look at herself to strengthen and develop a style personality we call "elegant," which instantly shows how much you take care for yourself, how thoughtfully you choose your wardrobe, how important quality is for you, and how responsible you are.

What is the keyword for your industry?

🐦 Sylvie di Giusto @Sylvie_diGiusto

"Every career path has some kind of uniform that signals that you belong in this position or to this industry." #TheImageOfLeadership

Chapter 5
Leaders Look Professional

 Jeff Belle @jeff_belle
"You can't be it, if you can't see it!"
#TheImageOfLeadership

Everyone agrees that leaders have to look professional. Your professional appearance (at least at work) certainly can make or break you and your career. If you want to be perceived as competent, as someone who has a purpose, who is important and serious about the things you do, you might want to act like a professional in everything you do—including your wardrobe choices.

Looking professional can be related to living within the appropriate dress code. And many people tell me that finding the right dress code level is difficult, especially because there are so many unspoken dress code rules.

No, it's not difficult. It's quite simple, because there are no "unspoken" rules. To the contrary, they are very outspoken and clear. There are certain colors, fabrics, and patterns that are allowed in each dress code level and not in others. While this is not a "how-to" book, we need to describe those levels a little bit, because otherwise we're not describing what "professional" actually means.

Here are the five Dress Code Levels of business attire:

DRESS CODE LEVEL 1: BOARDROOM ATTIRE. For a male professional, boardroom attire is limited to a black, navy blue, or charcoal suit; a white shirt; and a discreet tie in a modest color, plain or with a very subtle pattern. Black shoes only, Oxfords or Derbys, probably with a cap toe, and high-quality accessories including the wristwatch and attaché case. Less is more. This is the attire you choose if you are a member of the highest level of any governing body, private or public (or, if you are about to meet a member of the boardroom). No exceptions. The rules are pretty much the same for women—which means a classic two-piece suit with a white blouse, an elegant pair of black closed-toe pumps, and without any doubt, no matter the seasons, pantyhose. Of course.

DRESS CODE LEVEL 2: TRADITIONAL BUSINESS ATTIRE. It gets a little bit more flexible with traditional business attire, which is the attire we have to wear on a daily basis in our offices. As a male professional you can add pinstripes to our suits, white shirts can be replaced with bright blue ones, ties can be more colorful or patterned, and shoes might even be allowed in a dark brown tone. However, it's still a very ambitious and high-level dress code. Same again is true for women, who can add more color to their suits or shirt blouses and even choose a nude or colored pump. Bad news—still no open toes and still no excuse to skip the pantyhose.

DRESS CODE LEVEL 3: EXECUTIVE CASUAL. Here professionals are allowed to wear slacks and sports coats, and choose patterned fabrics and more colors. It's obviously getting more relaxed. Men can skip their ties or change them for a trendy woolen one. Monk-strapped shoes or elegant loafers can be worn. Women can add unique accessories and show their individuality by wearing bright colors and fabrics. At this level it would be the first time I'd maybe consider an open toe shoe. Sigh—you still need pantyhose. But never together with an open toe!

DRESS CODE LEVEL 4: MAINSTREAM CASUAL. Men can skip the formal dress shirt and wear a more casual shirt, maybe even combined with a sleeveless sweater. Men still would wear it with a pair of slacks and combined with shoes that are very much relaxed but elegant. Women can exchange their blouse shirts to tops, even with short sleeves, although I'd still recommend wearing a vest with it. And finally, pantyhose are not tremendously important.

DRESS CODE LEVEL 5: BASELINE CASUAL. For those who aspire any kind of leadership responsibility, this dress code level doesn't really have any relevance. It's what you might wear in a private environment, certainly not at the office. For an executive, it may be appropriate at a rustic corporate retreat with outdoor activities. Basically, you can choose whatever you want to as long as it is clean and in shape. Let me explain it with the pair of denims, another very common question related to dress codes. Yes, this is the dress code level that allows you to wear denims at work. However, we're talking about a clean, dark, elegant pair of jeans, and not the washed-out version with fabric holes or other signs that it's worn out, whether on purpose or not.

🐦 Sylvie di Giusto @Sylvie_diGiusto

"Your professional appearance (at least at work) certainly can make or break you and your career." #TheImageOfLeadership

The +1 / -1 Rule

On a daily basis, it's quite easy to choose the right dress code for the occasion. The first thing you should do is to determine the dress code level you're currently in. What do you think? Which dress code level is appropriate and right for the position you currently have? In general, I advise professionals to dress one level higher in the future (+1). Don't jump two levels up, because you'll look overdressed, and never jump down. Why? Because we want to dress like the leader we want to be, right? "Look like the leader you want to be, long before you are one."

If for any reason you can dress down (it's a seminar at work, casual Friday, an office party, or a home office day), I recommend that you never dress down more than one level (-1).

If you stay within the +1/-1 rule you never risk being underdressed or overdressed. It's also the reason that the CEO of a company who dresses usually in Dress Code Level 2 will appear in Level 3 at the leadership training seminar, which is his or her interpretation of "going casual." They probably won't appear in Level 5 because it doesn't even exist in their understanding of professional office attire. Someone who usually works in Level 4 instead might look very casual when he or she goes down to Level 5.

Furthermore, another rule of thumb is: the more you deal with a client's money, with their life, their future or their family, the more traditional and conservative you should be dressed. People like this usually work in finance, law, accounting, insurance, health care, real estate industries. A more casual dress code can be chosen when you are a leader in an industry as information technology, travel, manufacturing or education. People in creative industries instead—fashion, public relations, multimedia, entertainment, advertising, marketing—should be more innovative and creative, and can go for the latest trends. Those might be found in a very high dress code level, or in a more casual one. They very often combine both.

It used to be easy to get dressed for work. Put on a suit, add a shirt and tie or blouse and jewelry, and you were ready to go. Not so today. The introduction of "business casual" has been a mixed blessing, adding more comfort and creativity along with confusion and chaos. While dress code policies explain every detail about professional business attire (and have been vented and practiced over many years), there has been less or little effort to explain a casual dress code to employees. Business casual is not meant to be sloppy; in fact there are many rules you have to follow to dress accordingly and still respectfully.

Too many people think casual means that you don't have to care. Wrong. Casual means that just a few single pieces of your business attire are different; the rest remains within your regular dress code level.

Furthermore, the challenge of dressing business casual is to not become too casual in other areas of work. Just as I believe "You are what you eat," so "You are what you wear." Recent studies have indicated that employee morale and productivity are, in fact, no better when a dress-down policy is in place. In fact, many of my clients have told me they are revising their dress codes back to traditional business dress.

🐦 **Sylvie di Giusto @Sylvie_diGiusto**

"The more you deal with a client's money, the more traditional and conservative you should be dressed." #TheImageOfLeadership

Politicians and the Dress Code

Here's a nuanced political example. President Obama is generally at Dress Code Level 1. If he wants to go casual in public, his way is to not suddenly wear khakis and a polo shirt. He takes off his jacket, rolls up his shirtsleeves, and removes his tie. That's it. It's still the power suit he is wearing, but he just went -1 on the scale to show his casual interpretation of a president's dress code. He did not swap his Level 1 suit for something more casual; instead, he removed the jacket and tie. It's Level 1, casual.

When attending casual events at military installations, to maintain his Level 1 dress President Obama wears a classic Type A-2 leather flight jacket in combination with his white dress shirt and suit pants. The A-2 has become a popular presidential garment; both George W. Bush and Barack Obama have worn them in photo ops at military installations.

Mitt Romney chose another way to dress casually during his 2012 run for president. He was quite often seen in high-waisted jeans, khakis, and a casual shirt without a tie. With this outfit he steps down several steps on my +1/-1 scale. What this outfit says is: "I'm one of you. I'm an 'everyman.'" And by the way, this is a message many Republican candidates in general seem to follow when it comes to casual dressing, spearheaded by former president George W. Bush, often seen in his casual pair of jeans. But there is some irony of the presidential image and appearance as a leader: We want a president who looks polished, powerful and strong on the one hand, but voters also want someone they can relate to. (Which voters will relate to someone with rolled up sleeves in a power suit, and which voters will relate to khaki pants?). And in addition, while we want presidents (and leaders) always look energetic, fresh, alert and brisk, we also want to see them hard-working and exhausted. This is a challenge also faced by many leaders in corporate environments. On the one hand, their team members want them to be someone they can look up to, while on the other hand they want them to be one of them—although he or she will never be.

To come back to Mitt Romney's example, and his choice of going casual and showing "I'm an everyman." The truth is, if you paid close attention to his jeans you could see that they obviously were professionally pressed. What it says is, "Even when I dress casually, it's in a very controlled way." I'm a perfectionist. I'm in control of everything. Even the crease of my pants.

And that just runs quite against and counter to the idea of being an "everyman."

His avoidance of the Level 1 boardroom suit was obvious from the first day that he announced his candidacy in June 2011. As Kurt Soller on Esquire.com reported, "For his announcement speech, Romney showed up in a baggy tattersall shirt. His sleeves were neither rolled to his elbows nor buttoned at his wrist. Instead, they were stalled on his forearms, the sort of move a man makes when he goes to roll his sleeves but gets distracted by a sandwich. Again, there was no tie. And on his waist, he chose a hokey silver-tipped belt, one that's a bit too long, yet still manages to hold up his baggy, pleated, black pants.

"Then, of course, the hair. 'It looks a little looser. It doesn't look as tapered off, and it's not as plastered with product to look shiny,' says Rodney Cutler, the expert in these matters, who called after the speech. 'You don't want to look unapproachable, and this is definitely going to appeal to the masses.' So: Grow your hair, lose the suit, ditch the tie, and perhaps you'll be ready for the country's highest office too."

Clearly, Romney's wardrobe pivot was an effort to soften his image as a Bain Capital corporate raider whose personal net worth is estimated at $250 million, dwarfing that of Barack Obama, who today banks roughly twelve million dollars, mostly from book royalties.

Here's another example. During the 2012 campaign, presidential candidate Rick Santorum became well known not just for his conservative politics but his trademark sweater vest, a phenomenon that happened almost by accident. "Amazing thing that sweater vest," he said. "It happened on a night I was doing an event for Mike Huckabee in Des Moines. I showed up and everybody was in shirts and ties, and I showed up in a sweater vest. Turned out I gave a pretty good speech that night, and all of a sudden the Twitterverse went wild, saying it must be the sweater vest." The mania picked up after a video called "Sleeves Slow Me Down" went viral over the weekend. That came after the vest acquired a Twitter feed of its own, @FearRicksVest, and a Tumblr under the same name. The obsession with the wardrobe choice of the eventual second-place winner in the Iowa caucus was not surprising. Commentators focus on fashion when they've run out of more substantial topics to cover. We're in a twenty-four-hour news cycle, and just about every topic in the political realm is rehashed over and over again. The slightest anomaly receives the white-hot glare of the media.

Rick Santorum's sweater vest is just one of many efforts politicians have made to connect with the common voter. In the 1996 presidential campaign, Lamar Alexander wore plaid shirts, denoting his identification with the everyman. When Scott Brown ran his senatorial campaign in Massachusetts to fill Ted Kennedy's empty seat, he sported a barn jacket and drove a red pickup truck.

I remind political candidates that the smallest detail is important, because the last thing you want is voters becoming distracted by something you wear, something you do, how you look, or how you behave. The moment people talk about something like that—hair, eyeglasses, weight—usually there is something wrong with it.

Anyone paying attention to Hillary Clinton after February 2013, when she retired from her four-year stint as secretary of state, would have noticed a change in her appearance. As a globetrotting diplomat, she often looked just plain tired and worn out. During a CNN interview she boldly stated that she did not have "time to worry about putting on makeup." She was probably right! But soon after leaving office, her public appearances revealed a new attention to basic image issues such as hair and makeup. Many in the political sphere were claiming that one of the main target points for Republican campaign managers in 2016 would be the idea that the former secretary of state, who will be sixty-nine years old on election day 2016, would be too old to run for president. In December 2013, Barbara Walters pointedly asked Clinton if her age was "a concern." She answered that no, it was not. Then Meghan Daum of the *Los Angeles Times* explained that while more rest might result in Clinton looking "less jowly," she "cannot be presumed to maintain her past and current energy levels into her seventies." Daum urged Clinton supporters to admit the "devastating" truth: "2008 was their one and only chance, and they missed it."

Despite her recent image makeover, there are those within the Democratic Party who worry that her road-warrior appearance will come back to hurt her if she does run for president. The attack ads practically write themselves: "Do we want a president who cannot even endure the demands of being secretary of state? How can we turn the nation over to someone like that?" Or alternatively, "Do we want a president who represents herself like this to the outside world?"

When interviewed by CNN, Hillary Clinton stated that as the "have pantsuit, will travel" globetrotter, she stopped worrying about the reaction to her appearance, suggesting that if she wanted to wear glasses, she would wear her glasses, and if she wanted to tie her hair back, she would tie her hair back. Despite having said that before, after becoming a private citizen she clearly changed her mind. In fact, at the CFDA (Council of Fashion Designers of America) Awards held in June 2013, she not only wore makeup and styled her hair in such a way that it flattered her, but she even referenced her previous fashion choices (or lack thereof) in a joking manner. Clinton, there to present the Eleanor Lambert founder's award to her friend Oscar de la Renta, had no trouble bringing the entire auditorium to its feet. Wearing a midnight blue glittering pantsuit by Oscar de la Renta, Clinton said, "Now that I have some more time on my hands, I am going to be pitching Andy Cohen and others on a new show for Bravo TV to sort of fill that gap that is so apparent to some of us. We could call it 'Project Pantsuit.'"

The crowd went wild.

As our political culture is increasingly dominated by visual communication, especially in political campaigns whose durations are measured not in months but in years, the nonverbal takeaway rises to eighty to ninety percent of the communication.

"Whether it's Santorum's sweater vest, Sarah Palin's glasses, or Hillary Clinton's pant suit, political fashion can serve to tell us something about the candidate," said Catherine Wilson, assistant professor of political science at Villanova University, in the *Christian Science Monitor.*

When political fashion works well, such as Hillary Clinton's pant suits, it serves as a candidate's professional trademark. When it goes wrong, such as the "Mission Accomplished" episode when President George W. Bush dressed in a flight suit on the deck of the USS *Abraham Lincoln* and declared an end to major military operations in Iraq, it dramatizes an already controversial event. In these cases candidates can't avoid being drawn into discussions of fashion.

Political campaigns are rife with examples of the good, the bad, and the disastrous fashion choices. In 1988, Democratic candidate Paul Simon's well-known bowtie summed up the public's understanding of the former senator from Illinois. He was seen as being a bit of a nerdy intellectual, and the bowtie confirmed it. While supporters liked the tie, and handed out bowtie pins at events, voters were cool.

Disastrous wardrobe choices can take on a negative life of their own. In 1988, when presidential candidate Michael Dukakis toured a General Dynamics facility in Sterling Heights, Michigan, he was invited to ride in a 68-ton M1A1 Abrams Main Battle Tank. The visit, meant to support the candidate's credibility as a future commander-in-chief, became one of the worst campaign backfires in history when Dukakis put on a huge helmet and rode around in the tank. It pretty much ended his campaign. The image of the oversized military headgear completely overwhelming the man reinforced belief among voters that he was too wimpy to be commander-in-chief.

Presidents have learned to avoid any type of costume, and to this day the infamous Dukakis tank ride is invoked any time a politician declines to put hats on their heads—as President Obama did when he was handed a Navy football helmet but refused to try it on. ("You don't put stuff on your head if you're president," he said. "That's politics 101.")

🐦 **Sylvie di Giusto @Sylvie_diGiusto**

"The last thing you want is people becoming distracted by something you wear, or something you do." #TheImageOfLeadership

When Dress Codes Don't Count

Yes, there are those special occasions that make it a little bit harder to choose the right dress code. But that's the reason they are "special." In general, I recommend dressing within the +1/-1 rule while adapting to the dress code of the host.

When Chris Christie toured his state after Hurricane Sandy, he wore the famous fleece sweater. Did this follow any dress code level for a governor? No, of course not. A fleece sweater of this kind doesn't exist on my five-level dress code concept.

But it was the right thing to wear for that specific occasion.

The challenge with dress codes is not that there are unspoken rules. The challenge is that people misuse clothes for the wrong purpose or occasion. Some people would wear that sweater when there had been no hurricane. They "misuse" clothes and the occasion.

I tell people that flip-flops were originally made for the beach, right? So why should I wear flip-flops anywhere else than on the beach? Unless you work on the beach and your job is being a lifeguard, flip-flops just have nothing to do in a professional environment.

The same is true for yoga pants. Yoga pants are for yoga classes. Why should I wear them outside of yoga classes? Most yoga pants have never seen the inside of a yoga class. Sport shoes are made for the gym, as well as sweat shirts or sports jerseys. So why would you wear them anywhere else when they were actually made for the gym?

With leather pants you should rock on a rock concert, and sequins and glitter are made to add some great shine and effects due to disco light. And as the term already says, *underwear* is made to be worn *under* your clothes. So why should anyone see it?

If you don't have to shovel a tremendous amount of snow, Uggs are not the right choice for your office.

And how about Crocs? Sorry—I would say the only purpose for which Crocs are made is to fill the trashcan.

And then, of course, there are many who think those rules are true only as long as they're at work, and as long as they're getting paid for the hours spent accepting the burden the company puts on you by asking you to be dressed appropriately, and to interact and communicate professionally.

Here's the truth: It's just half of the story.

Many companies that face a battle with their employees, and sometimes even with their management crew, hire me because those people believe they have the right to dress, to behave, and to interact in a way that suits their own individual personalities. It is their personal "right" to look however they want and to do whatever they want in any way they desire. And yes, you might agree that this is basically true—outside of the employer's four walls.

But many companies also know that their employees have to be aware that the way they present themselves can send intended or unintended messages to others around the clock. There are countless incidents—we could all tell dozens of stories—of people who have created an indelible negative unprofessional imprint in our heads by a weird wardrobe choice, or just by one click: the inappropriate tweet, that awkward picture on Facebook, that doubtful fetish they live out on Pinterest. They damage their own reputations by ignoring the fundamental laws of the Internet: everybody can hunt you down online, and nowadays first impressions are often made long before we enter a room to meet someone.

In our professional profiles we're encouraged to include photographs of ourselves, especially now that social media and connectivity are more popular and important than ever before. However, the portrait you get by taking a quick selfie with your smartphone is not going to send the same professional message as a quality headshot. The difference is noticeable, and it shows that you are serious. Especially if you consider that your pictures are on the Internet forever, you want them to be high quality.

> 🐦 **Jo Saunders @JoAtWildfire**
>
> "Use your profile photo on LinkedIn to start a conversation not end one."
>
> #TheImageOfLeadership

They also ignore that they can damage their employer's reputation. Why? Review what you read about confirmation bias in Chapter 2.

Social media was never intended for this; it's another misuse, just in a digital way. It wasn't invented to comment, discuss your job, your boss, or your working conditions online. And instead of seeing this as a an intervention or an interference in your fundamental personal

> 🐦 **John Michael Morgan @johnmorgan**
>
> "If the people who complain all of the time online do the same offline, I feel sorry for those they live with."
>
> #TheImageOfLeadership

rights, I encourage people to see it as a guidance, as a helping tool, as a part of a quite important deal: You don't want to comment, discuss, or publish your personal things on the corporate intranet either, do you? They do the same; your employer has to act professionally in regard to your personal life within or outside those four walls. All they expect from you is to be part of this deal, and they even give you guidance through dress code rules and regulations.

A professional image can easily be damaged at after-hour events. I work with female leaders who when at work wear the most traditional, classic, and conservative pieces, and who arrive for an evening event in inappropriate mini dresses. Those women's credibility and integrity suddenly becomes a question, even if they're not in the office. I once had the pleasure of taking a group of young talented potentials on a sailing cruise for a team training program. For whatever reason, some of them assumed we'd spend the entire program dressed in bikinis and flip-flops. They simply forgot that such events are still official functions of the organization they worked for.

Rules and regulations count anytime and everywhere, both for yourself and for your employer.

I encourage you to see those rules and regulations not as a burden but as valuable tools that help you eliminate confusion. They help you to shape the image you would like to project for yourself and for your company. It's a leadership skill to accept basic rules, and to value that there is guidance out there, given the fact that drafting a dress code rule is pretty far down on most employer's list of things to do, since many of them think that adults shouldn't need dress code guidance. And in some way I do understand it, because it's simply common sense. It's not nuclear science. Whenever somebody is in doubt if this or that piece is appropriate to wear at work, trust me: When in doubt, it probably isn't.

🐦 **Sylvie di Giusto @Sylvie_diGiusto**

"Whenever somebody is in doubt if a piece is appropriate to wear at work, trust me: When in doubt, it probably isn't." #TheImageOfLeadership

Chapter 6
Leaders Look Respectful

 Summer Silvery @_sumerae
"The way you respect yourself
sets the standards on how
others will respect you."
#TheImageOfLeadership

Leadership is a matter of both showing and earning respect. Do you agree? Most leaders do.

Well, so is a dress code. Dressing appropriately is a matter of respect as well.

I see respect from two different perspectives. First, you have to show respect for yourself. Second, while it's important for your self-esteem, showing respect for yourself makes people believe that you also have the ability to show respect to others. Most of us want to be respected by others. This is true not only in our private lives, but also at work.

When I consult companies in order to create new or to improve their existing written dress code rules, "respect" is something I recommend to mention at the very beginning of their policy. Because it's something we all desire, it's something each and every one of us wants at work, and it's a requirement most people have within their career: I want to be respected.

🐦 **Jeff Sherman**
@shermanspeaks
"Respect is preventative medicine."
#TheImageOfLeadership

Therefore it's easier to tell them straight ahead that the company dress code policy will help each and every employee to feel respectful for themselves and to earn the respect they desire.

It's a Sign of Self-Respect

The most important person in your career is not your boss. It's not the boss of your boss either, and it's not the HR recruiter. It's you. You are the CEO of your career and you are the champion of your success. Therefore, I encourage you to start with yourself.

One of the easiest and most effective ways is to dress respectfully. This does not necessarily mean expensive suits, luxury jewelry, or designer high heels instead of cheap finds at the outlet center. Not to everyone. It does not mean slicked-back hair instead of curly waves. Not to everyone. Dressing with respect might look different on every single one of us, and that's just an amazing thing.

Remember, there is no one-size-fits-all formula for leaders. But there is one thing all leaders have in common: they respect themselves. This means first and foremost that they are willing to invest time and effort into themselves. They give some thought to their own bodies, to their day's activities, to the people they are going to meet before choosing an outfit in the morning and while grooming themselves in their bathrooms. While looking into their mirrors they are aware that it's not going to be the last time they see the output of these efforts today.

> 🐦 **3DConsultsExecutiveD**
> **@3DConsultsExecD**
> "First, dress your heart. It's amazing what internal glow does for an outfit." #TheImageOfLeadership

The person you see most often every day is yourself. So show yourself some respect and invest in yourself.

When talking about a professional demeanor, I want to stress that it's about more than just being physically attractive. Your body, your mind and your health are three determining factors when it comes to showing up for work every day. Drinking enough water and eating a healthy diet are important, and you want to make sure that you get enough sleep and enough exercise. It will not only make you healthier physically, but also make you clearer mentally. To both improve your own feelings of self-worth and stay healthy, you need to set aside time and pamper yourself.

> 🐦 **Dawn Gallagher**
> **@YourHomeSpa**
> "Successful leaders do not think of taking care of themselves to be expensive, self-indulgent, or time-consuming."
> #TheImageOfLeadership

Get a degree, become certified in your field, take classes outside of your field, or learn another language. Make sure that you stay up to date on the news in your field and that you know what the major talking points are. These ensure that others see you as someone who is determined and hard working. You'll be someone who is in the know, and who increases your overall value to your employer.

Back to your clothes. No matter how much you took care of your favorite twenty-year-old coat or ten-year-old suit, at some point you've to toss it.

The Image of Leadership by Sylvie di Giusto

You can hold on to the past, or you can create your own professional imprint today. As a leader you want to be perceived as someone who is up to date, right? No matter how much you like those comfortable old black pants and white blouse, there's no good reason to wear the same thing every day, five days a week. As a leader you want to be perceived as someone creative, innovative, risk-taking, and more resourceful than a five-day-the-same-look.

Does that mean you should go fashion crazy? No. The truth is that it's better to say "no thanks" to the hottest and newest fashion trends. The corporate world doesn't expect you to be at the top of the fashion curve. In fact you probably shouldn't be. This doesn't mean that you have to lose all your individuality. You still can implement a sense of fashion into your outfits. But start with small touches. Build smart basic wardrobe modules and add that little bit of fashion personality.

"Does it have to be expensive?" is what you probably think right now. The truth is, that nearly every business leader I know—male or female— is well dressed, and it's never cheap. At some point in your career you simply need to understand that you cannot move forward by shopping for professional clothing at Target. "You are better than Target!" is something I tell my clients straightforwardly.

> 🐦 **Joel Thomas**
> **@joalericthomas**
> "I have to help my clients to see that they are worth it. From there everything falls into place."
> #TheImageOfLeadership

Don't get me wrong; I don't want to unfairly malign a big and successful company. I could use any other retail company with a similar price structure. And believe me, I'm happy to shop at Target for many of the things I need around the house. But when it comes to your profession-al imprint—that critical seven seconds during which you absolutely must make a positive impression—I call upon my clients' self-respect.

Say it: "I… am… better… than… Target.

Instead, I want you to buy expensive, I want you to buy smart, and yes, I also want you to buy cheap. Let's start with the expensive pieces in your wardrobe: Investment pieces are timeless pieces in your wardrobe. They will help you to never be at a loss for what to wear, no matter the occasion. They are the perfect pieces because they offer you versatility. They send out signals like, "I'm ready for serious business." In my experience, those are usually not the cheap ones. In fact, you might have to invest in a custom-made suit, a fitted blazer, an elegant overcoat, a great handbag, or that perfect pair of black Manolo Blahnik heels. Like I do when I wear them for important meetings or presentations. Again, it doesn't mean that it has to be Manolo—not to everyone. It just means it to me, and you will also find me in cheap twenty-five-dollar flats with studs, just because I wanted to jump on that summer trend 2013. Imagine I would wear them this year. Everyone would roll their eyes and think: "It's so 2013." In terms of fly-by-night fashion trends, I recommend to find cheap ways to get these must-have pieces for the current season. However, with investment pieces you should follow the "one-third" rule: Buy one-third as many clothes as you do now, but spend three times as much on each item.

Buying "smart" simply means that you look for more affordable ways to buy your investment pieces, which is great as long as you don't skimp on quality. Bargains are everywhere, you just have to look for them: buy them out of the season, at sample sales, on online flash sale sites, in outlet centers or consignment stores, or use apps which inform you when your favorite investment pieces go on sale.

And sometimes, you even don't need new clothes—you just need better *fitting* clothes.

How many times have you seen attractive people in clothes that are totally the wrong size for them?

Your professional appearance and attitude is an investment, not a burden. There's an ROI on professional appearance, and anyone who aspires to leadership needs to understand that.

A positive first impression will only open the door. It's up to you to make a sustained effort, day after day, week after week, to live up to your self-created professional imprint. Respect is earned over time, in countless inter-actions under a variety of situations. Anyone who has run for high political office knows this. You're on the campaign trail for months, living under a spotlight, with every action and word intensely scrutinized. You need to maintain your professional imprint every moment of every day. Sure enough, others around you will mess up—they'll say something stupid, or appear on an embarrass-ing photo. This is part of the test that candidates need to go through before voters will cast their votes for them. It's a sustained and long-term investment of time and energy into earning the respect of the people around you.

🐦 **Sarah D'Alexander**
@dalexands

"Give respect even if you don't get it in return."

#TheImageOfLeadership

Remember that even if you're moving along your career path smoothly, it's not just a luxury to invest in yourself; it's a necessity. It's a sign of how much you value and respect yourself. Fortunately, self-confidence will grow out of self-respect.

🐦 Sylvie di Giusto @Sylvie_diGiusto
"The person you see most often every day is yourself. So show yourself some respect."
#TheImageOfLeadership

It Shows That You Respect Others

Yes, each of us wants to be respected for our genius mind and our great character.

Absolutely right. So why would you do anything to distract from these valuable assets? Just saying. Period.

Otherwise, you risk ending up being the one wearing a lime green pant suit among a group of crisp white shirts, like Hillary Clinton did during her G20 group photo on February 21, 2012, where she stood out from the crowd as the only participant not dressed in white. It gave us all a good laugh, even shared by Hillary and the other people in the picture, no doubt. But the problem for Hillary was that the press was full of articles, headlined that she obviously didn't receive the "white shirt memo." Many people will remember this *faux pas*. But the public might not remember which important decisions this group has made during this G20 meeting. Instead, the lack of preparation on the part of her team made her appearance a topic.

My personal view on this was it showed a lack of respect. She and her team allowed her appearance to become a topic, instead of the important content of the meeting.

🐦 Susan Pierce Jacobsen @AmFamSusan
"If we are remembered for what we are wearing, we may have chosen the wrong outfit."
#TheImageOfLeadership

I once saw a professional speaker wearing a shirt on stage with a saying on it. I don't remember a word he said (I even don't remember his name), but I do remember the words on his shirt: "Sorry Ladies, I'm Getting Married." Good for you, fella!

Or, let's talk about Rob Ford, who insists he'll be re-elected as the mayor of Toronto. Many articles have been written about him, and I do not want to get to deep into his actions, because most people understand that smoking crack cocaine—and then being videotaped while doing so—is not a great career move. However, it's interesting to watch how he handles his endless mistakes, how he communicates about them, and how he appears while suggesting that everything until now has been either a tremendous misunderstanding or a plot to discredit him. Despite the fact that Rob Ford has a right to wear whatever he wants (or, maybe he hasn't, given the fact that he represents the people of Toronto, Canada's largest city), when he wears the jersey of the Toronto Argonauts football team while apologizing for inappropriate sexual remarks, or a cheap, shiny, black-red magician ensemble with a huge, dirty spot on the shoulder and is sweating profusely while appearing in front of millions of viewers of the Jimmy Kimmel show, what it really says is: I am a clown. I do not care about myself—or about you, your expectations, or your perception of me.

While one would certainly have to admire his chutzpah, it does not work for the mayor of the largest city in Canada. In order to get things done as a mayor, it is important to build bridges, to appease certain people, and to work with individuals even when you do not necessarily agree with their message. In other words, as a leader it's important that you care about what others think, and that you confront them in a respectful way.

We all have those memories of people who stood out from the crowd, unfortunately for the wrong reasons. In my trainings, many participants share their own awkward stories about friends, pals, bosses, clients. Usually I respond with questions about the person they are talking about, related to the job interview or appointment they met him or her; facts and figures is what I try to find out. More often than not they are not able to answer my questions.

🐦 **Kathy Kiely @MadamePrez**
"Let your words and not your wardrobe be what they remember."
#TheImageOfLeadership

It's like every other relevant or non-relevant information about this person has been washed out from their memory; left is only the *one* awkward reason they remember this person.

Many of those stories have in common: A lack of respect for the occasion. Why do we wear suits for job interviews, at least in the majority of cases? Why do we brush our teeth after eating food? Why do we wear black for

The Image of Leadership by Sylvie di Giusto

a funeral, a dress for a wedding, something conservative at the White House? We do it out of respect. Respect for religion, culture and all kinds of human beings.

When Jay-Z and Beyoncé met the president of the United States, as a sign of respect they showed up in a perfectly tailored suit and an appropriate dress, while when performing for their respective audiences—whether or not the audience includes the president—both of them jump into very different, very un-presidential stage outfits.

🐦 **Jacqueline Peros**
@jmbranding
"Image starts with what's inside. Being civil towards others is the foundation to achieving an indelible personal brand."
#TheImageOfLeadership

The same president wears something on his wrist that has become the most "watched watch" in the world. President Barack Obama appears in media throughout the entire world, and he often rolls up his sleeves, which makes sure his watch catches the eyes of even those who are not usually "watch spotters." And for those who missed it newspapers, magazines and blogs make sure you know the story of Obama's "Secret Service watch," which he received from his Secret Service staff as a present for his forty-sixth birthday. Comparable chronographs can be found for around 350 dollars. While for some of us this is already a quite expensive way to decorate your wrist joint, others might be surprised that the president of the United States doesn't wear a more expensive watch. It's part of his public image. It shows how much he values and respects the people who surround him and take care for him and his family. For the similar reasons Michelle Obama regularly wows us with clothes from young aspiring, sometimes even unknown American designers, instead of going for the big names within the fashion industry.

When you think about New York's former Mayor Michael Bloomberg—whose net worth is thirty-three billion dollars—you probably wouldn't think he gets his corporate-executive uniform of navy pinstripe suit, crisp shirt, and understated blue silk ties in one of oldest, darkest fabric buildings in Brooklyn. While he obviously could afford to choose more fashionable, more luxurious, more reputable designers and tailors to create his clothes, he frequents Martin Greenfield in his dumpy warehouse, who also counts ex-President Bill Clinton, former US Secretary of State Colin Powell, and former New York Police Commissioner Raymond Kelly along his clients.

Recently the Duchess of Cambridge, Kate Middleton, has shown that she is nothing if not thoughtful about her choices picking items that have a contextual relevance to the even she's at or the country she's in. Pictures of her went around the world when she picked a white lace dress by from an Australian designer for her visit at Sidney's Olympic Park.

You might think about other cultures, philosophies, or religions whatever you like. But when you choose to interact with them, you'll be much more warmly received—and respected—if it's clear that you've made an effort to appreciate the local customs.

🐦 **Vaibhav Pandya**
@pandyavaibh

"I'm not concerned with your liking or disliking me. All I ask is that you respect me as a human being."
#TheImageOfLeadership

One of the places I've seen the most completely inappropriately dressed people is Dubai. Considering Dubai is much more relaxed than other UAE States it's really not hard to follow some of their basic rules. In a nutshell, while you are out in public you should have your skin covered from shoulders to knees. Bare chests are not allowed in public, nor are clothes that are see through. So far I didn't mention anything that is not also true for a corporate office in America, right?

It really sends a message of a lack of respect and that you don't care where you and they are. Choosing the appropriate wardrobe is a communication skill. It's not a burden, because if you are smart you can also use it to send important positive messages.

This can go so far that Thomas Barrack, CEO of Colony Capital, said in a *Wall Street Journal* interview that he wears pocket squares only in London and doesn't wear an overcoat in Paris, where men don't wear them. In New York he ties a scarf one way, and in Italy another, so as not to be seen as an outsider. The article also mentions Donald Trump, who tries to mirror what other people in a given situation are likely to be wearing. His aim seems to be to eliminate distractions. (Personally, I'm not sure if he always reaches that goal).

You might not want to go so far that you've to analyze the fashionable and historical details of pocket squares and overcoats. All you have to do is to follow a few points of etiquette and show your respect to others. Prepare, put some thoughts into it, and analyze what the expectations are and what your host, your colleagues, and other participants might wear.

Can it ever be too much? Can you go too far? Indeed you can, no doubt. You shouldn't wear Emirati native clothing just because you travel to Dubai.

The Image of Leadership by Sylvie di Giusto

And yes, in every training that I lead we have a discussion about being overdressed or trying too hard, which I absolutely understand and which indeed can happen. But does the corporate world have a challenge with people who are overdressed? No. The opposite is true. I have insight into many corporations worldwide, and believe me when I say this: I cannot think of one person or one company that has ever hired me because they were facing the challenge of their staff being overdressed, or trying it too hard.

A safe route to go is to create something I call a "uniform of respect." Just find something that's always professional and appropriate. In many training sessions, participants come up with cases where while they work in the technology industry, they sometimes need to meet financial advisers, and how they would adjust their wardrobe for such meetings. Doctors who meet lawyers, Southerners who meet Westerners, non-leaders who meet leaders—the cases and examples are far-reaching and inventive. And while participants consider they have to adjust their wardrobe every time, a simple and easy way is to create a wardrobe that works for all those cases. A "uniform of respect."

This is what President Barack Obama has done. His basic suit, shirt, and tie combination work just about anywhere.

In the area of entertainment, Jimmy Fallon is an excellent example. When he's on the screen during the *Tonight Show*, you won't see him in anything other than in a perfectly fitted suit, with a simple white or bright shirt and an elegant tie. This suit is so perfectly tailored to his specific frame that you simply can't do much better. It just shows how much time and effort he, his tailor, his manager, his stylist, his production company —whoever—is willing to invest into his appearance. It shows the self-respect he has for himself, as well as for his audience by inviting them into his "virtual" living room and wearing the best possible suit he has to welcome us. From First Lady Michelle Obama to singer Snoop Dogg, this is an outfit that just works with everyone. Regardless of who takes their place in his guest seat, he never adjusts his wardrobe to the person; he has simply created a "uniform of respect." And although you might not see the details immediately, he even shows respect to his crewmembers. Those wardrobe choices are nothing less than absolutely media friendly, from being balanced with the background color of his blue curtain, over never wearing pinstripes or small patterns that would create an unpleasant moiré effect, to avoiding high contrasts. These are all the things that lighting technicians, cameramen, and video editors like to see and to work with, given the specific challenges of the television medium.

Because when you're on stage—a TV studio, a speaker's platform, presenting in the front of a meeting room, or sitting across from your job interviewer—when you're "on stage" you are welcoming the eyes of everyone in your audience. So many studies have shown that while we may want to pay attention to the message, a garbled presentation will cause confusion. Whether you're speaking publically or convincing a potential employer that you'd be perfect for a high-level management position, respect matters if you want to convince the audience or keep your image aligned with your message.

And while motivational speaker Tony Robbins might give amazingly positive speeches, it's hard to look at him and not see him as a person who borrowed a friend's suit at the last minute because he realized he was due to go on stage. And I think to myself, "That's it? That's what you came up with this morning, when you went through your daily activities, noticing you'll soon meet hundreds of people?"

I know what you're thinking: "Tony Robbins is a highly successful expert! He doesn't need to worry about what he's wearing." Yes, indeed he is; I'm not questioning his skills, his knowledge, or his expertise. However, speaking directly to every aspiring leader, I'll say very clearly that you need to believe that an ill-fitting suit doesn't mark you as an expert, but as a beginner, and as someone who has just discovered there is more to style than cargo pants and flip-flops.

I want you to keep your audience's attention; and the easiest way is to avoid distraction at any price, every day. Create a wardrobe of respect and just ask yourself every morning: Would I feel comfortable meeting the CEO down the hallway any time today?'

🐦 Carol Davidson
@CarolDavidson
"It's never just about the clothes... It's what the clothes say about you."
#TheImageOfLeadership

🐦 Sylvie di Giusto @Sylvie_diGiusto
"Keep your audience's attention, and the easiest way is to avoid distraction at any price, every day. #TheImageOfLeadership

Chapter 7
Leaders Look
Controlled

 Bruce Van Horn @BruceVH
"Self-care is not selfish! You
cannot properly care for
others if you are struggling
to care for yourself."
#TheImageOfLeadership

E ndless stories have been written about the many things that successful C-level executives do at the break of dawn. From working out at the gym (in preparation for a half-marathon, of course), to mapping out the day and recording that day's personal and business goals into their smart phones, flipping through the hottest business news, putting on their neatest suit before giving a quick interview over the webcam, to a fresh, light and of course organic breakfast with their beautiful wives and children. They seem to work a full day even before they hit the morning rush hour. You might think they are superhuman—but of course we all know they are not.

What they want us to *think* is that they have everything under control. While they see the "big picture," they don't lose sight of solid ground. And while we still think about whether we would be able to do all those things, they *just do it*. And they do it right. They don't do it by halves. Leaders don't like semi-finished projects right? They like action, discipline, and results. Leaders want to cross the finish line.

Living in New York is like being part of a giant fashion show. One of my favorite spots and pastimes is people-watching at the Federal Hall on Wall Street. I sit next to George Washington's giant statue and absorb the "image of Wall Street". Things are usually good from afar, but far from good when I look a little bit closer.

🐦 **Kristie Kennedy**
@kristieykennedy
"To reap rewards of sweet success, one must sow seeds of sour discipline."
#TheImageOfLeadership

Not all of the successful and powerful Wall Street leaders walking by pay attention to detail. They might think nobody notices, but I do notice—a random person sitting on the stairs of Federal Hall.

You can wear the best-fitted and most expensive suit, but without proper grooming and care of both your body and your clothing, you will not look your best, and will not be perceived as a leader. Why? Because you are not in control of both your body and your clothing. No matter how fab the coat, the bag, the dress—if you've two inch roots, or you are walking on the nails of your high heels, it simply doesn't work. It's all in the details. Repeat after me: "It's all in the details!"

Take Control of Your Body

As of this writing, one of the reasons people are relatively unconcerned about Chris Christie's weight in view of him being a possible candidate for the most important job in this country is actually not the weight itself (the number of pounds he carries, or the number of pounds he has lost). It's that he consistently shows *action*, generally with quite impressive consequences. He gets in control and he takes over the driver's seat. He does everything needed, and even more than most expected, to show he can be disciplined and controlled.

Compared to this, let me quote his fellow New Jersey politician Cory Booker, the current mayor of Newark, who has said that he immediately gains weight if everything's not running smoothly. He once told *Menswear*, "I was so stressed, with massive layoffs and terrible police negotiations, I gained fifty pounds." He has a constant history of gaining and losing weight. While he's a talented person and rising political star, that doesn't sound like someone who has himself, particularly his weight, under control or is disciplined, right? It's usually not what we want to hear from leaders. Self-control and self-discipline is a must for leaders. If you can't organize yourself, your ability to have others follow you is very doubtful. Successful leaders are usually highly self-controlled, they have a tremendous sense of organization, inner calm, and resolve.

You know some examples of people who aren't? Are they really successful in a long term? Think about it again.

Back to Cory Booker and his weakness of uncontrolled weight gain and loss. Don't judge too quickly. He does something many successful leaders do, which is to maximize his leadership appearance by shaving his head. If a man's hair starts thinning—which by the way is something most men face at some point in their lives—it's a good idea to just shave it. You simply show that it's you who controls this process, not your hair. Researchers at the University of Pennsylvania's Wharton Business School confirm this theory and found that while those with male pattern baldness may have low self-esteem, men who preemptively shave their heads are seen as having more leadership potential. This is because they appear more dominant, and because *they* control the process, not their hair. They've made the decision, not their hair. They are in the driver's seat, not their hair. They control their hair; their hair does not control them.

A totally unattractive alternative (other than to wear a hairpiece or get a hair transplant) is the dreaded comb-over, where the man tries to create a look of youthful fullness by layering long hair over the balding cranium. This invariably looks unnatural and, if caught in a high wind, can blow apart and take on the appearance of a furry rodent prancing about on the man's head. Of course, the world's most famous comb-over belongs to real estate tycoon Donald Trump, so much so that his hair has practically become a New York tourist attraction. I don't know what Donald Trump looks like without the comb-over, or what he would look like if he shaved his head. It may be that his current hairstyle is the best possible solution for him.

In our society, a full head of hair (not necessarily long hair, but hair that covers the head) is seen as a sign of youth and vitality. Thinning hair is equated with a loss of vitality. Therefore, for many men, it's better to have no hair than to have bad hair. I tell them: "Don't fight it. Just shave it!"

If you're lucky enough to have a full head of hair, control of your hair is essential. Think of Howard Stern. The way Howard Stern presents himself is as though he just woke up one day and threw on whatever happened to be lying on the ground. His long, unkempt mane reflects this. While this certainly suits his "I do not care what anyone thinks of my controversial statements" persona that made him famous in his early days, we would probably not identify him as a potential leader for corporate America, right? Aside from the obvious ill-fitting outfits, it would not just work for him to throw on a bespoke suit. His hair is something he would probably have to get control over.

Then there's facial hair. Many men grow beards because they think it's fashionable, or makes them look more attractive or older. Unlike, for example, the nineteen-fifties, we live in an era in which it's perfectly fashionable for men to have facial hair—as long as you're not a business leader or politician. Why? It's again because of control. To keep a beard perfectly well groomed is just a really hard thing to do, and in fact most beards do not look well kept.

Yes, there are exceptions, of course. Steve Jobs grew a beard, and co-founder and chief executive officer of Oracle Larry Ellison has one. Marc Benioff from Salesforce, and Richard Branson of Virgin Group, all have beards. But these men are entrepreneurs who founded their own companies. They never had to apply for a job, and they never had to prove they were leaders. And in fact, be very honest with yourself when you Google one of their photos: Is it a beard that looks well groomed and controlled? I agree. I rarely meet leaders with well-trimmed beards and mustaches.

You'd think that it's just common sense to shave every day, or to take care of one's personal grooming. But the truth is, it's not. You'd also think my job as an image consultant involves only the obviously fashionable, great and fun things like expensive bespoke suits and shopping in luxury department stores. Of course, it does. But it also involves the part where I need to talk about things that are obviously not common sense in everyone's mind. There are those who just do not control and take care of their bodies at all, while there are others who overdo it.

I'm talking about a long list of grooming mistakes: offensive breath and yellow teeth, extensive sweating on the one hand, too much cologne or perfume on the other, smelling of stale smoke or odors caused by flatulence, dandruff on heads or flaky dry skin on the face, impure skin and blocked pores, fake tanning, hairs on necks, in ears, noses, on fingers and legs, patchy chest hair, electric-blue eye shadow or layers of wrong-colored foundation, dark circles around eyes, abnormal nail biting or overly long, false nails or elaborate nail art, simply unclean nails, piercings in eyebrows, noses and tongues, ear studs and stretched ear lobes over cosmetic or decorative tattoos, failed hair coloring experiments or undyed hair roots and hair lines, teased hair or hair plastered with hair gel slicked back, false eyelashes, false nails, false everything…

I've seen—and have had to address—it all. Over many years, I've worked with individuals and with organizations on their professional images, often as the "outside expert" brought in to deal with these delicate personal issues. And while all the companies I work for and all the participants I meet agree that those are important things and are common-sense topics, they still exist.

If you saw just one thing you do, have, or battle from the prior list, make sure you act immediately. Just do it! Now. It might be as simple as buying dandruff shampoo, using deodorant, changing the nail style, or skipping the self-tanner to seeing a doctor, because some of those examples are related to health issues. Just do it! Take control. No one will tell you, but I'm telling you that anything else will hurt your career.

This is not just my opinion. A recent survey called "Grooming at Workplace" released by the leading Indian staffing company TeamLease Services reported that eighty-nine percent respondents felt that "style of dressing has long term impact on overall image of an Individual." Good grooming—looking polished and put together—mattered most to the survey's respondents. The survey found that eighty-three percent of senior executives believed that "unkempt attire" detracts from a woman's executive presence, while seventy-five percent of senior execs believed it detracts from a man's.

How about whiter teeth? Results of a study conducted by an independent research firm provided evidence that an attractive white smile has a direct effect on successful interpersonal interactions, both socially and professionally. "The Impact of Whiter Teeth on Key First Impressions" study, commissioned by Crest Whitestrips, revealed that a whiter smile substantially affects how others think of you when you first meet.

And then there's perspiration. Some of the most embarrassing grooming issues in the workplace have to do a personal care basic—deodorant. Ninety-three percent of HR professionals in a recent Gillette survey said body odor or sweat stains are big red flags when it comes to meeting job candidates. Knowing that you're protected from sweat stains and body odor can help you maintain confidence.

So, did you identify anything on the list that might be true for you? Did check your breath? Don't be offended. Be glad it's me who tells you. Because another challenge with these personal issues is that people usually don't tell you if something is wrong. Instead, they tell others. Your professional and personal image—your reputation—is not always what people tell you it is. It's what they say behind your back.

Furthermore, they usually don't talk about things you're doing right. Instead, they enjoy talking about things that are wrong. And, honestly, if they start talking about something that's wrong, it usually is. Even if some might think it's just details, it's simply unnecessary if people judge you based on those little details instead of your excellent skills, knowledge, or experience.

Each of us has a message that we portray to the world. You either control what the message is, or you allow the world around you to make assumptions about what your message possibly is. A lack of attention to details immediately sends a message that you are uncontrolled or disorganized. People think leaders can't do great things at work if they don't feel good and look good. Successful leaders eat well, exercise, and care for the one thing that's their most important asset—their bodies. They are operating at the highest level of performance and control of themselves, and therefore they are able to do the same for their team members and their companies.

Take Control of Your Clothes

Taking control of your body is the first and very important step. However, it's not only how much you care about yourself, it's also how much you care about the clothes that cover your body. The logical next step, therefore, is to control your wardrobe.

Taking care of your clothes before, during, and after you wear them will not only make you look better, it also shows your leadership potential. Why? Again, because proper wardrobe maintenance requires control and discipline. An ongoing task, it requires that you carve time out of your busy business schedule. It's the same principle that is true for our CEO friend who goes to the gym at five in the morning.

Although a detail and just a small reflection of who you are, it shows the larger picture of the life you live. Many details together create a bigger picture: the shine of perfectly buffed shoes, the freshly pressed dress shirt, the unwrinkled suit jacket, the quality leather belt, the small but meaningful pin on your lapel—it's a reflection that you leave nothing to chance, that you control the professional imprint you want to leave on someone else's mind.

Here is one of the usual conversations I have with some of my clients. For example, I've seen so many wardrobes where the most expensive suits or dresses are hanging on cheap wire hangers, leftovers from their last cycle through the dry cleaners. Wire hangers are pretty useful when you lock your keys in your car. But certainly *not* in your closet.

My clients usually say to me, "Yes, I know," and nod their head in embarrassment. So if you know, why don't you just spend a little extra and purchase professional shirt, suit, and dress hangers? You might have to spend five or ten dollars for each, but this is a small price to pay to properly hang a two-thousand-dollar suit, right? Just do it!

I've seen C-level executives who use paper clips to fix their torn jacket lining or their suit pants since they've walked down the hem, or with missing suit jacket buttons and totally worn-down shoe soles. How much does it cost to bring a suit jacket to the tailor and fix the buttons? How much is it to bring your expensive pair of shoes to a cobbler? I mean, how expensive are lint rollers, mothballs or shoe trees?

They nod again, still embarrassed, but add, "It' not about the money, you know, it's about the time!"

I say, "C'mon, it takes only one minute to brush your suit jacket and trouser after each wear, before you hang them on professional hangers and air them out for the next time. It takes you one minute to order those hangers on the internet. It takes you one minute to use those shoes trees. Polishing your footwear is another one-minute job if you do it regularly. If you don't have time to do it, you've to outsource it. The same way you do it within your business when resources are not available. There are plenty of services, even online, that can help you with that. They even come to your doorstep to pick up your clothes and bring them to the dry cleaner, shoe cobbler or tailor. Might that be more expensive? Yes, it might. But you just told me—it's not about the money."

Patrick Allmond
@patrickallmond
"Don't be busy. Be productive."
#TheImageOfLeadership

It's just about *doing it*. And most successful leaders have one thing in common: At a certain point in their career, they have been "doers," and they just did things. Later, their responsibilities might not allow them to do it on their own; instead, they have the ability to find the right people and partner up with those who can do it for them.

Sylvie di Giusto @Sylvie_diGiusto
"The most successful leaders have one thing in common: At a certain point in their career, they have been 'doers'." #TheImageOfLeadership

Be prepared for the predictable and the unpredictable

It's not only about building your wardrobe and investing in quality items that may initially be a little bit more expensive, it's also about the way you use it, combine pieces, and accessories it. Paying attention to the visual details of your look conveys preparation, planning, and respect for those whom you meet.

You've got to determine your activities and responsibilities for that particular day, always keeping in mind your industry, your company's written (or unwritten) dress code policy, your position within the organization, and the people's requirements whom you are about to meet.

Before just throwing on something randomly, think about:

- What's the big picture for today?
- What's the occasion?
- With whom will you be interacting?
- What will they be wearing?
- What will your client be wearing?
- What will your audience be wearing?
- What will your boss be wearing?
- What will your colleagues be wearing?
- What will your team members be wearing?
- Where are you going to meet?
- Where are you possibly heading to after you've met?
- How will you get there?
- Who else could you randomly meet today?
- Which message do you have to deliver today?
- Is there any environmental risk you need to be prepared for, such as rain?

If you don't have the answer to those questions, you might have to do some research and become an "image detective." Google the people you are about to meet, find their profile pictures or visit their companies website. If you want them to respond well, you want to find out what they feel safe with, what they respect and admire. Your goal should be to fit in to their culture and requirements without blending in but standing out for the right reasons.

🐦 **Maureen Klecha**
@MaureenKlecha
"Believe that others will be happy to know you, expect that. If you don't feel this about yourself others never will."
#TheImageOfLeadership

Accessories, for example, can give you the final, subtle touch that will complete your professional appearance and image. Sometimes the choice of the right accessories not only has a fashionable reason and purpose, but a very practical one as well. Where do you carry around your coins? In your pants pocket? Or in an old chipped leather wallet? And where will you have your wallet during the day? Again, in your pants pocket? What do those bulges you create say about you and your two-thousand-dollar suit?

I remember a job applicant I interviewed when I worked for a German company. He said all the right things. At the interview's conclusion, he took out his iPhone to schedule a follow up meeting with us. As he searched through his calendar, I noticed an offensive word emblazoned on his phone's case. Immediately I found myself questioning everything I previously thought about him. We ended up hiring him, but he almost invalidated a great first impression with being careless with the choice of his accessories.

Or, I work with professional speakers. Dressing for the stage presents special challenges. Cameras are sensitive to colors, pattern and reflection. It's important that they take care of every little detail when they select their clothing and accessories to make sure they play well to the camera and the audience, and that they don't distract themselves as well.

Some speakers are not aware that their beautiful gold wristwatch is quite noisy every time they slam their hand down on the speaker's desk. They are not aware that the small-patterned tie, the thin-striped shirt, or the polka-dot dress are a challenge for the camera team. Those beautiful red-soled heels most ladies love are difficult too because they may reflect on the stage they're walking on. The shiny silver belt buckle, the ting-a-ling necklace next to the microphone, the distracting tie pin—every detail counts, and not only on stage. If your jewelry makes noise and jungles or clinks when you move, it's not the right choice for the workplace, because it's simply distracting.

One of my clients told me about the first annual performance feedback she ever received from her boss. It was quick, short and positive. However, he wished she wouldn't wear her annoying charm bracelet. Although he probably wanted her to leave with the impression that she did everything right and her performance was top-notch, she said she will forever keep this conversation in mind as one of the negative ones.

It's a matter of minutes and a few dollars to place a toothbrush in your office desk in order to avoid a breath problem that we all might have after a business lunch. A hand-held steamer might be the answer for your shirt if it needs a quick touch up. Have handy another pair of pantyhose, just in case your current one gets a run.

I'm sure you've heard it, and the timeless adages still holds true: "Success is where preparation and opportunity meet." Your best guarantee to achieve an image as successful leader is preparation. Preparation for predictable and unpredictable opportunities on your way.

> 🐦 Bryan Bumgardner
> @BryanBumgardner
> "Look like it took you three hours to get ready but act like you've forgotten what you're wearing. Effortless."
> #TheImageOfLeadership

> 🐦 Sylvie di Giusto @Sylvie_diGiusto
> "Success is where preparation and opportunity meet. Your best guarantee to a professional image is preparation." #TheImageOfLeadership

It's Not Only About Clothes

Fairly or not, the people who surround you, from your friends in real life to your friend list on Facebook, to those who tagged you on Instagram after last weekend's party, your family, including your parents and children, your husband or wife at the company's Christmas party, are all part of your image. You have allowed them to be part, or chosen to make them part of it.

For your own image it is important to surround yourself with people who are smart, driven and like-minded, and who reflect the

> 🐦 Emily Thomas @emitoms
> "There are two things you shouldn't waste your time on: things that don't matter and people that think you don't matter."
> #TheImageOfLeadership

person you want to be. Relationships should help you, not hurt you. Choose the people who surround you wisely. Friends, who you are proud to know, who you admire and who you respect.

Let's take another look on Chris Christie, who at the time of writing this book, still hadn't confirmed or denied his presidential run in 2016. Obviously he's ready for it, but is everyone around him on the same level? The answer to that is a resounding "No." Unfortunately for his wife, Mary Pat Christie, she has not yet shown the poise and composure necessary to be a First Lady and to appear the way Americans want a First Lady to appear. One example of this is the 2013 victory speech from Chris Christie. If you watch the speech, you can see a wide view of the entire Christie family. The only one who stands out is Mary Pat, but unfortunately not for the right reasons. Bright red is certainly a no-no if you are not scheduled to be the focus of attention. You can also see that she is having discussions with someone off-camera, moving around awkwardly and giggling, or sniggering during moments when there is nothing funny in the speech. For example, Michelle Obama clearly understands that most often she is not the main attraction at the president's speaking events; her husband is. This is the reason Michelle Obama downplays her features, while she still looks elegant and remains rather modest in her appearance. She manages to remain classy while also fading into the background, because this is about her husband, whom the people voted into the highest political office in the United States.

Back to Mary Pat. While it may sound harsh, this speech was a resounding success on all levels—except for her. She appears disinterested in the scene before her and does not seem to realize or recognize the momentous occasion that is transpiring.

Remember that this speech is one of the most important speeches in her husband's political career yet. Mary Pat seems to be oblivious to what is going on around her and cannot maintain professional poise for a mere eighteen minutes. The American audience wants someone who shows that they are in the moment, who understands how important it is to be calm and collected during the important moments—and Mary Pat is clearly not yet that person.

Presumably, the next speech to carry the same level of importance will be the one during which Chris Christie announces that he will be seeking the Republican nomination for 2016. Some people will ask whether it is fair to critique a potential First Lady, especially given that this is an extra-constitutional office (meaning that according to the United States Constitution there are no parameters for the First Lady's role, duties, or power). Some people even go so far as to ask if we should

🐦 **Gordana Biernat**

@Powertalk

"You can not control others, but you can control how their energy affects you."

#TheImageOfLeadership

"protect" Mary Pat from criticism. Of course it's fair to critique her; the truth is that if Chris Christie is going to run in 2016, he is doing so with his wife, family members, and everyone who surrounds him. They are part of his image, like an accessory he carries around.

Who are the people that surround you on a regular base? They have an influence on how successful you will be. Because, it doesn't matter how great you are, it doesn't matter how talented you are, it doesn't matter what your position or title is. All that counts is that you are surrounded by people that will help and support you. People who are worth spending time with them.

A car is not an accessory that you wear either, but it certainly is the kind of accessory you take to a business function. It's a statement of your values. Do you drive a Prius? A Cadillac Escalade? A BMW? A minivan? Your car sends a message about who you are and what's important to you. How you take care of your car is a reflection about you as well. Is it cluttered? Is it dirty? Treat your car as another potential part of your professional image and show how much you care.

Take a walk around your office today and consider the different office desks. What do you see? How do they look? What's the first impression they make when you enter the room? I hope you share my cut-and-dried and rather low opinion, which is based on thousands of desktops I've seen, of those people who clutter their desks with family photos, plants, post-its, clocks, calendars, coffee mugs, stacks of papers, a guest chair buried under a pile of jackets and handbags, and souvenirs from past travels. An entire collage? From best friends, to cousins, to grandmas and uncles? And children, of course, children in the "funniest" and "saddest" moments ever, accompanied by colorful first scribbles and writings. All of this says that you cannot wait to finish work and get back to your real life with family and friends.

By all means, I'm not telling you that you can't put a family picture on your desk. But look at the desk of a leader, maybe your CEO or any C-level leader in your organization. They very often have one family picture standing on their desk, beautifully framed, from a professional photographer; and their beautiful spouse is smiling at them while holding their even more beautiful children. It stands on their otherwise spotless desk like a trophy, like something he or she has achieved, even next to their demanding jobs and responsibilities.

Research shows that the owner of the organized and uncluttered desk has higher chance of getting a promotion. Sam Gosling, professor of psychology at the University of Texas, says, "A messy desk suggests that its occupant is not conscientious, a trait that is one of the biggest predictors of success." There are personality traits that can get you promoted, such as responsibility, initiative, and organization. And your desk, being a direct reflection of you, sends subconscious messages to superiors.

According to another survey of over one thousand workers by the staffing firm Adecco, fifty-seven percent of Americans admit they judge their co-workers on the basis of how tidy or messy they keep their workspaces. Nearly half reveal they have been "appalled" by how sloppy a colleagues' office is, and most attribute the mess to nothing more than laziness.

"With so many open office plans today, more people can see into your workspace, and they do judge," said Jennie Dede, vice president of recruiting for Adecco. "It's often personal. They think that you must be a slob in your real life."

A similar report by OfficeMax revealed that office clutter undermines motivation and productivity. "Your performance coincides with your workspace," said Dede. "When it's organized and precise you have the mindset and motivation to work."

🐦 **Heidi Deblaere @hdeblaere**
"Managing your image is about recognizing the genuine aspects of yourself that should come across to other people."
#TheImageOfLeadership

You might think that controlling your image is simply a form of micro-management. Yes, to a certain point, it is. But from the outside perspective it means that you take care that every single detail is well thought-out.

Maybe it's time to look around and clean up your wardrobe—and your car and your desk. Possibly, even some friends. Do it! Just do it!

🐦 **Sylvie di Giusto @Sylvie_diGiusto**
"You might think that controlling your image is simply a form of micro-management. Yes, to a certain point, it is." #TheImageOfLeadership

Chapter 8
The Challenges of Female and Male Leaders

 Pilar L. Davis Media
@pilardavismedia
"Professional image is like a book, make sure the cover reflects the quality of the story inside."
#TheImageOfLeadership

While you've been reading this book, you may be thinking about that loaded word, "stereotype," of which the dictionary definition is, "a conventional, formulaic, and oversimplified conception, opinion, or image—one that is regarded as embodying or conforming to a set image or type."

From very early in our life, one lesson, which we all learn is that stereotyping is bad, bad, bad.

I disagree. Not because I think stereotyping is good, good, good. I just wouldn't generalize it that way.

Stereotyping provides humans with the ability to quickly sort out patterns in a randomly diverse world filled with people of every size, shape, gender, age, color, and sexual orientation. And it's just a quick first pass, nothing more. It gives people a pattern they can use to understand, learn, and grow. This positive characteristic of stereotyping can quickly turn negative when it leads to pre-judgment as an end unto itself. Then it's bad, bad, bad.

As image consultants, it's part of our business to stereotype. We have to open boxes to demonstrate our clients how they are possibly perceived by others. We work with boxes labeled with "tall," "petite," "old," or "young" and have to show quite plainly how the world possibly thinks about you if you are part of this box. It's not judgmental, though. Stereotyping simply says that there is a box labeled with "overweight" and that people may perceive you as a low-performer. Judgment says that every overweight person is a low performer.

Stereotyping means that I show pictures of the same woman, Amber Heard, once with dyed peroxide blond and once with natural brunette hair, and ask participants which of those women they believe is more intelligent. Responses are usually made with one voice. If you leave my seminar with the thought that every blonde must be dumb, it's not a stereotype, it's a judgment.

Therefore, without judging anybody, I would like to share some stereotypes with you. Specific groups of people, stereotyped "boxes" and the related challenges that I most often observe when working them.

Let's start with my female clients, before I share an insight into my male clientele with you. In terms of their appearance, women usually face a much harder challenge than men. Because men have to meet relatively simple standards of professional appearance, both in the United States and worldwide: business suit, dress shirt, necktie. In contrast, any creative choice that a woman makes often will be criticized—too conservative, too trendy, too colorful, too tight, too loose—just because it doesn't fit into the stereotyped picture of the two-piece power suit.

Here are some of the ways that women can go off course.

The Tinkerbell Challenge

We all know them—those nice women who flutter around the office. Always happy, always smiling, and exuding a positive aura, with some magical sprinkles too. The soft voice, the soft handshake. She usually nods her head to the side when she giggles, making her look like she would be a little embarrassed about this oh-so-grown-up joke. She is the first one who raises her hand if someone asks who will get coffee for the meeting, so she can easily trip through the conference room door—since she anyway doesn't look forward to possibly standing up in front of the crowd and presenting last months results. What is she wearing? If you can't image her right now, please read again in Chapter 4 what my oh-so-cute client was wearing.

Why don't Tinkerbells get promoted? Because they appear to be overly emotional. Because companies fear that with the slightest threat of a challenge, they'll either burst out in tears or just flutter away. And if they get promoted? And face the slightest hint of leadership challenge? They'll burst out in tears or flutter away.

My answer to this dilemma? There is no answer other than: Stop being cute!

The Kardashian Challenge

You know what I'm talking about. This type of woman requires no explanation. We all recognize her; she's very intense in her tight dresses and high heels. And usually she shows a lot of skin. She moves and acts as if there were cameras recording every gesture for broadcast to the masses. She's not living; she's performing.

Why is it that Kardashians don't often get promoted? Because they don't give anybody a chance to see their brains. Instead they show everything else. Usually, it's too much skin, it's too much make-up, it's too much jewelry, it's too much heel, it's too much of everything except fabric. And because they distract with all those "too much" things, only a few people actually notice that their might be quite an intelligent, creative, reliable, or trustworthy person behind the elaborate façade.

And if they get promoted? It doesn't get any easier for them, because people still think they "earned" their promotion not because of their excellent leadership, but because of their bodies (that all the other girls would like to have).

My answer to this dilemma? Very simple: make your choice. You cannot have it both ways. If you want to be a sex object, then be a sex object, but don't get in a snit when people—both men and women—think that's all you've got. And by the way, women can be just as judgmental to other women as men are. In the workplace, your Kardashian bump-and-grind routine will turn off other women, too. Let them see your brain first, your heart, your character, your inside. Give them the chance to see through your clothes, because your clothes do not distract in any way from the inside. If you want to be known for your inside, make sure it's what they actually see and notice first.

The Cold-As-a-Fish Challenge

They are tough, they are strong, they are powerful, and they stand above everything. No emotions, no friends, no partnerships; they just focus on results, results, results. They are part of the imaginary boys' club, desperate to be accepted as members by the big boys, because they play "their game". It usually implicates long working hours, forsaking oneself for the price of a career. They tend to dress masculine like their supposedly teammates, wear less makeup, usually don't color their hair, look not approachable, don't show anything personal or anything that would reveal there is actually a beating heart inside the power suit. She doesn't want to be kind; in fact she despises Tinkerbell. She might surround herself with Tinkerbells, because they tend to please her, but she would also fire a Tinkerbell in the blink of an eye.

Why they don't get promoted? Oh, don't worry—they do. But only to a certain position, to a certain level in the organization. Because what they forget is, that the boys in the boys' club know exactly how she works. They know they need someone in the hierarchy below them who "fights" on their own authority. They need them exactly where they are and nowhere else—as a partner in crime during every combat. Cold-as-a-fish-women get ahead; don't worry. But most often they are just used by others who misuse their unemotional focus on results, and who would ever think, maybe because those boys in the boys' club recognize that leadership is not simply a matter of acting tough.

My answer to this dilemma? Recognize that leadership knows no gender. There are both men and women who are unsuited for top leadership roles because all they know is "my way or the highway." Keep all the good traits you already have, just make sure you make many friends on your own along the way. At one point in your career (and it's going to be exactly the point where you don't get further ahead, because your own boss doesn't want you), you'll need this network.

The Schrute Challenge

We've all seen *The Office*. As brilliantly portrayed by Rainn Wilson, Dwight Schrute is one of the show's most memorable characters. He's a "weirdo." He dresses weird, he behaves weird, he communicates weird. We recognize his character for his many flaws and idiosyncrasies: his lack of social skills or common sense, his love for weapons and the justice system, his many attempts to get promoted, and his rivalry with fellow salesman Jim Halpert, played by James Duncan.

Schrutes are easily identifiable by their appearance: a weird haircut, with awful bangs, big sideburns, thick eye glasses, a double-pleated corduroys pants with a telephone holder attached to the belt. Usually they carry something around that seems to be not from this century, or not from this world.

What most people don't remember, though, is that in every season Dwight Schrute has always been the highest-ranking salesman with the best results at Dunder Mifflin.

Why do Schrutes don't get promoted? For many reasons. One of them is that people simply don't identify them as leaders, because their fabulous and groundbreaking performance doesn't get noticed. Or simply because they are ticking time bombs. Obviously they don't control themselves, and others just fear, "What's next?"

And if a Schrute does get promoted? In reality, they very often get something I call a "fake promotion." Their leaders are aware of the great performance those people often deliver behind and beside their weird appearance and behavior. They don't want to let those results go, and, driven by their own personal agenda, they want to profit as long as possible, while accepting they have this weirdo in their team. Therefore, they create fake positions and fake promotions for them. Promotions that don't exist on any organization chart. Just remember in how many seasons Dwight Schrute, the best sales manager in the branch, became the second or third in command as assistant to the assistant to the regional manager.

My answer to this dilemma? "Un-weird" yourself as much as possible. Get in tune with the culture of your office. Be a team player. Have respect for the people you work with, even if you think they're a bunch of drab and colorless drones.

The Superman Challenge

They are everywhere, because everywhere there's someone or something they have to take care of. And if there is anybody who can take care of a problem, it's them. They exercise in the gym, and have a perfectly toned body and white shiny teeth that you notice every time they have a smile on their lightly tanned face. Great hair, manicured nails, shiny shoes, expensive watch, powerful walk in their well-fitted suits—and still they hire me, the image consultant. Why? Because they want confirmation. They approach me with the high-value idea that they want to learn, look for advancement, and become "perfect." But the truth is, they think they're already perfect. After all, they're supermen. Right?

Why is it that supermen don't get promoted? Oh, goodness, they do. They do all the time. Usually, too often. Because very quickly, when it comes down to the slow and steady grind of producing measurable results, supermen face challenges. The numbers can only be inflated for a certain amount of time. The moment others (or they themselves) figure out that the performance behind the superman costume is not according the performance they're expected to deliver, they take off to rescue another project, team, or company. They just take off.

My answer to this dilemma? Every company needs supermen and superwomen. In fact, many of them, and consistently. The thing is, the true super heroes look like ordinary people who know how to put in the hours, day after day, week after week. *Consistency* is the keyword.

Oh, yes—and please don't hire me. I'm not very good at confirming that you're a hero.

The Men in Grey Challenge

Published in 1973, *Momo*, also known as *The Men in Grey*, is a German fantasy novel by Michael Ende. It's about the concept of time and how it is used by humans in modern society. It's a story about time-thieves and about Momo, the little girl who brought the stolen time back to the people. When the novel finally hit the big screen, the movie visualized how those time-thieves looked like. Grey hair, grey tint, grey suits, grey everything— they looked tired, sick, weak, and de-energized. Simply grey.

I see them in real life. Often they wear some kind of uninspired grey suit, with a sad tie, old worn-out shoes, and an old belt. They look like the corporate world has sucked out their last bit of energy; and the sad thing is, they really don't mind. Amazingly, because they are not aware of their greyness, only a few of them become my clients. They spend years and years in the same position, possibly get promoted at one point, and don't get promoted again for many years. What they don't understand is that their non-energetic aura is contagious; it sucks out the energy and time of others.

Why don't Men in Grey get promoted? Because they are colorless and don't stand out, at least not for the right reasons. They are invisible and overlooked. Not only do they get ignored, but nobody wants to mingle with them.

My answer to this dilemma? Start living! Do something adventurous. Break out of your comfort zone. Get into colors. Show others that you are alive. Demonstrate there is energy in your spirit and your soul.

Is it fair that we create those stereotypes? Maybe; maybe not. It just happens, because most brains need patterns to think in and to work with.

Only a few of us work effectively and at a high performance level within an environment of chaos. Is it fair to judge others with these stereotypes? Probably not. But it reflects how the world works. When it comes to your professional imprint, the seven-second rule is reality. Do they give us any other chance? Probably not, that's also true.

🐦 **Nic @stylebrute**
"You need to frame your story before others frame it for you."
#TheImageOfLeadership

Rick Genest is a Canadian artist, actor, and fashion model, better known with his stage name "Zombie Boy". Tattooed on his entire body to resemble a living skeleton, Zombie Boy has worked in various freak shows across the world as an illustrated man, fakir, geek, and clown. He has been featured in many magazines and runs major fashion shows, and he also appeared with Lady Gaga in the music video for her track "Born This Way."

Zombie Boy also became part of a campaign entitled "Go Beyond the Cover," which promoted Dermablend, a professional makeup product. In the video you see an average looking guy, who is Zombie Boy with all the tattoos on his head, torso, arms, and part of his back covered by the makeup. The video shows him sitting, with the phrase "How do you judge a book?" He then proceeds to remove portions of the makeup, starting with a section of his chest to reveal the tattoo underneath, continuing to his face. The commercial success of this campaign has been huge. And he earned applause for showing the world that you cannot judge the quality, character, or skills of someone or something just by looking at it, by its cover.

It's quite wrong, because this is not fair. He tries to make people believe that anyone should see anything in him, from the reliable lawyer he might be, over the caring pre-school teacher, to the genius software developer. No, it's not possible. His cover says I'm Zombie Boy, tattooed as a living skeleton, and although you might wish to judge me as a caring, loving, fun, entertaining and giggling babysitter for your toddler, your toddler is probably scared of me. Some people simply don't give you a chance to look beyond the cover.

We all do it. We can't help. We are visual creatures—the visual area of our brains comprises thirty percent of our cortex.

But the great thing is, we also do it in the positive sense. It's true for those books and covers and people who draw our positive attention, create an expectation that excites us, and suggest a certain quality, character, and skill. I want you to stand out for the right reason. Yes, I want people to judge you by your cover—just because it's an excellent one.

Sylvie di Giusto @Sylvie_diGiusto
"I want people to judge you by your cover—just because it's an excellent one."
#TheImageOfLeadership

Chapter 9
Leaders Lead by Example

 Mark Sanborn
@Mark_Sanborn
"Every day you are building your
legacy whether you think about it
or not." #TheImageOfLeadership

Your most important job in your leadership role is to create more leaders. And great leaders lead by example. By walking the talk, you become a leader others want to follow. As a leader you set example for those in the lower hierarchies of your company, who always—I repeat, always—watch how their leaders appear, behave and communicate.

I encourage each and everyone who leads a team to set the direction by creating a best possible professional image for their own, because action simply speaks louder than words. It's like an unspoken standard, an unspoken dress code, grooming and behavior policy, and possibly much more effective than any written one. Your followers will watch, learn and imitate what you do, and it's one of the many opportunities the difference between a true leader and a no matter how great manager comes to the surface.

🐦 **Faith Rim @FaithTheModGirl**
"True leaders lead with zeal and are a constant example to others in their speech, dress & conduct."
#TheImageOfLeadership

Leaders provide guidance; they motivate and inspire people to take action, most often by their own actions.

On the contrary, managers operate tactically. People will indeed follow the manager's instructions and do what they are told do for many reasons, such as the fear of losing their own job. Managers hand out the written dress code policy, or brief their employees shortly about the main expectations how they have to appear, behave and communicate at work. Their message is: "Do it as I say it ..."

Leaders who lead by example instead are those great individuals who demonstrate the right way to go, who act as role model and who inspire others. Without actually saying it, their message is: "Do it as I do it ..."

Look at your fingernails. Are they dirty? Do you follow the company's dress code rule? What about your shoes? When did you check your breath the last time? How do you behave when you enter your company's door? What will I find on Google about you? Practice what you preach! You're always setting an example for every single person around you at every moment. Make sure it's a good one.

🐦 **Sylvie di Giusto @Sylvie_diGiusto**
"You're always setting an example for every single person around you at every moment. Make sure it's a good one." #TheImageOfLeadership

There Ain't No Excuse for an Unprofessional Appearance

The flip side, being a poor role model, is the easiest way to undermine your own authority as a leader. Does hat mean you have to follow all the rules (and burdens) your company puts on you? Maybe. Does that mean you can't have your own style, you can't stand out and show your personality? Absolutely not.

Influential leaders are confident, and they trust themselves enough to live their own interpretation of a professional imprint and image. They have put so much thought into it and created a very defined image, that their presence is instantly felt when they walk into the room.

🐦 **Milena Joy @milenajoy**
"If you are not memorable, you are replaceable."
#TheImageOfLeadership

They are mindful of how others could perceive them, and of how they want to be perceived by others. If part of this image building requires them to wear denims, they wear denims. If wearing sneakers to their suit adds something unique to their defined image, they wear sneakers. If they don't care about pantyhose, they really just don't care. No questions, no doubts, no excuses.

Instead, it's often those who are unsettled or insecure on many different levels, who pull me aside during or after trainings and ask me whether it's truly necessary for women to wear pantyhose, and can they get away with wearing open-toed shoes? For men, what about short-sleeve dress shirts or as mentioned denims?

The truth is that for most women, wearing open-toe heels to the office will probably not ruin their professional career. As long as you make a good overall impression, chances are that that little *faux pas* can be forgiven and will probably be overseen anyway. However, the problem is that if people get away with one thing, they are likely to attempt to get away with more. Soon the open-toed shoes may be accompanied with an open back, deep neckline, and rising hem.

What these people would like to hear is that there are exceptions for their specific situation. The answer is invariably "No." Upon hearing this, they immediately start to look for excuses. One of my favorite ones is the weather. It's either too cold to wear this or that, or too hot, or not cold or not hot enough, too dry or too wet, too windy or too whatever.

> **Sarah D'Alexander**
> **@dalexands**
> "Show confidence by admitting mistakes."
> #TheImageOfLeadership

But courageous leaders don't make excuses. They apologize in case they have done something wrong. And usually people have the most respect for those who don't hesitate to say "I'm sorry," or simply "I was wrong."

But people have a hard time respecting those who look for excuses in advance. A leader makes commitments, not excuses. If employees see commitment, courage and taking responsibility for the actions and choices leaders have made, it feels safe to them and right to follow that person.

I know a thorough leader who wears cowboy boots, around the clock. No matter where he is, no matter whom he is about to meet. It's part of his image, and he makes sure it is. Everybody knows who he is, and what he stands for; and the most influential business leaders don't care when he enters their boardroom in cowboy boots. Don't you dare think he doesn't care about his shoes. And don't ever think he is wearing these boots because he can't afford a pair of luxury Oxfords. (They are luxury hand-made bespoke boots, who perfectly shine and match his otherwise perfect fitting and wisely chosen outfit.) It's also not because they might be more comfortable.

> **Phil Graham @philgrahambiz**
> "There are people in expensive suits barely scraping by & hoodies making billions (and vice versa)."
> #TheImageOfLeadership

In fact, they are part of his well-thought through and elaborated professional and personal image. It's just one little detail that contributes to the imprint he wants to leave on their minds—as the fearless "boardroom cowboy." And I'm happy and honored to say that he agreed to write the foreword for this book; because Jeffrey Hayzlett demonstrates everything I describe within *The Image of Leadership*. He stands for it, always and everywhere, and you might be surprised that I encourage you to do the same.

If you want to dress up to go to McDonalds, by all means do it. If you make sneakers your statement piece at the office, please go for it. Don't sacrifice yourself just because somebody else has a problem with it. I truly believe that you can stand out for the right reasons, even with sneakers or cowboy boots, just because you are true to yourself and you made it a consistent signature piece of your image. Do it! Go for it!

Just don't be surprised if others follow you, and take the same right for themselves. Leaders lead by example, right. Managers instead make sure there are non-breakable rules others have to follow.

🐦 **Cesar Pinzon @CesarPinz**

"No matter how you dress, the leader sets the top end of dress code."
#TheImageOfLeadership

The challenge with rules is anyway that if you give people rules they automatically look for exceptions. It's our brain that is trained for this behavior. Some of us seem to exercise it more than others. When people see a street sign that says "Parking prohibited on Sundays," some instantly accept this rule without questioning. Others immediately focus on the other six days of the week and scrutinize the requirements for Monday to Friday, or even how they could possibly bypass them.

Are you curious? Do you want to hear what I hear nearly every day? Here are my top ten excuses for inappropriate appearance:

1. It's too hot. It's too cold. It's the weather.
2. It's too much money.
3. I feel guilty investing the money in professional attire.
4. I don't have the time.
5. My look is still working for me.
6. I have no sense for style.
7. He or she does it as well.
8. We're in the suburbs. This isn't Manhattan.
9. I don't want to lose my individuality by wearing what everyone else does.
10. It's just the Internet. Who cares what I look like?

Honestly, there are many reasons why you should wear something or should not, but none of them are related to the weather.

When it comes to the overall evaluation of whether you are leadership material, your habit of coming to work dressed professionally *every day* may make the difference.

It's as simple as that: Neither the weather nor the time or money you might have to invest are excuses for an unprofessional appearance. If you want to be different and stand out, do it! Just do it, but don't use any excuses. There simply are no excuses for you to appear unprofessional. The same is true for others.

But wait—if it's not you who's dressed inappropriately, if it's someone else—how will you tell?

🐦 **Sylvie di Giusto @Sylvie_diGiusto**

"Neither the weather nor the time or money you might have to invest are excuses for an unprofessional appearance." #TheImageOfLeadership

The Leader's Challenge: It's Not You, It's Someone Else

One of my duties as an image consultant is to be honest with my clients, the participants in my training sessions, and the people I coach. It falls upon me to tell them the truth about their body features, their speaking voice, their attitude and manners, their grooming, their personal hygiene... and therefore sometimes their bad breath. These are the kind of conversations that can make every leader's knees shake.

You might be surprised, but it's easy for me to do this. Because, I'm an external person, and one of my fellow image consultants once said, "We're in the *business* of body odor. You aren't."

While it might be an easy conversation for me, it can be a very difficult conversation for both you and the person with whom you discuss the problem. I want you to keep this in mind. It's not only difficult for you; it's even more difficult for him or her. Most leaders are as uncomfortable providing feedback about an employee's personal dress or habits as the person receiving the feedback. Why? Simply because it's something personal.

In my training sessions I challenge leaders by pairing them up, and without any preparation or warning I show one of them a card containing a task, such as, "He/She has very offensive bad breath," "He/She has very offensive body odor," "He/She picks his/her nose in public", or "He/She is dressed too sexy today." And so on. Most participants start the conversation with, "Jane (or Jim), I have to talk to you about something, and I don't want you to take it personally…" Well, it *is* personal. It's an embarrassing personal issue. You are entering a personal space that you are usually not called upon to enter as a leader. Therefore, be aware of the fact that the other person will in fact take it personally.

Best advice? Be sensitive. Handle the issue with respect for your employee. Master the leadership art of empathy. And of course, without any doubt, this has to be a discrete, private, and one-on-one conversation.

Is there one golden rule? Is there one winning statement with well-chosen words I can give you? No, unfortunately there isn't. This is because every employee is different, every relationship between a leader and his or her employee is different, every problem is different, and whatever the cause for this problem and the consequences for you, your team and your company is different as well.

Prevention has to be woven into all aspects of leadership. Reflecting a professional image is just another example how beneficial prevention could possibly be. It starts with leading by example, followed by paying extreme attention to the importance of a professional appearance at the first moment your new employee passes the company's doors. It's just one of the many chances you might miss to avoid these common problems.

🐦 **Michael Shuttlesworth**
@Manstoolbox

"Leadership is an accumulation of experience and the courage to use it for the good of others!"

#TheImageOfLeadership

"Talk to them!" It's as simple as that. Too often I get hired by companies who provide their employees with well-thought-out written and detailed dress code policies. In good faith, they hope that each and every one will follow the rules, which are explained down to the last detail. The truth is, they don't follow—for many reasons. Because they didn't read it, because they read but ignored it. Because they read between the lines, while you wanted them to only read the lines. Because they are masters of interpretation…

Written rules are often kept vague and nebulous, consciously or not. By just emailing or handing out a print of your company's dress code policy, you do not (I repeat, do not) prevent any willful or non-willful misconduct, you are just fulfilling one of your manager duties. As a leader you've to take time and invest into prevention, and this possibly means that you have to sit down and explain them exactly how you, your company and possibly your clients interpret the rules and requirements of your policy.

At this point I usually show a picture of Kim Kardashian in my trainings. In terms of her makeup she follows all the rules you might find in a written dress code policy that requires a natural makeup at work. Think about it again. Kim Kardashian? Natural? How could this possibly fit together?

If prevention failed and you might get into the difficult area of personal hygiene challenges, it may be helpful to start with an indirect, a soft approach, and you can do a few things before you address the topic directly. Handing out mints on a regular basis, or installing a small basket with deodorant sprays, disposable toothbrushes, or lint rollers might work. Sometimes people pretend to have experienced the issue on their own and simply find a way to talk about it. Will it solve your problem? Maybe. For sure? Maybe not. But, if not, it might at least show you if the person is aware of the challenge, which can make a huge difference for you during the conversation. Like the person who wears too much cologne, people are often not aware of the extent of the problem.

If you find yourself still lost with the challenge, preparation for a possible tough conversation is key. This ranges from simply gather the facts and figures to discussing the challenges with your Human Resources department. With facts and figures I mean the many measurable impacts and consequences an unprofessional appearance might have. Hand washing is critical to help prevent the spread of illness. Chewing on your nails will do the opposite if you handle food.

For the conversation itself, just keep in mind to be sensitive and respectful. The very first words out of your mouth must be, "Jane (or Jim), you are a valued member of our team. We love having you working with us, and your contributions are significant." You must start on a positive note so that the person doesn't get the impression that you dislike them or are looking for a reason to get rid of them. You really want them to succeed!

🐦 **Daniel Wallen**
@TheWallenWay
"It is good to be honest without hesitation, but try to present your thoughts with a positive spirit."
#TheImageOfLeadership

Acknowledge that you understand it might be difficult for the employee to hear, but don't share that it's hard for you to give this feedback. (First of all, this conversation is not about you, right? It's about them. And second, it undercuts your standing as a leader when you appear to complain about difficult duties.)

I recommend referring to the impact on the person's career and the ability to interact with co-workers or customers. I do not recommend using complains from others (no matter if they have really happened or not) as the cause and motive for this conversation. By referring to others who have identified or noticed the issue, you admit that you obviously haven't been aware of it in the first place. Or you have, but you didn't act instantly. Furthermore, making a big deal out of this situation, and saying that even others have complained, may make them sweat even more. Anyway, keep it short and simple, don't use qualifying words. Simple describe the issue and that you ask the person to handle it, or come back to you if help is needed to figure out how it can be solved. "That's all. Let's get back to work, Jane (or Jim)."

Accept any kind of reaction from your employee. This ranges from apologies to aggressive defensiveness, and even religious or health-based reasons you might have not thought about.

Most people thankfully will try to remedy the issue if they realize it has been noticed by others. While they may at first be surprised or even offended, more often than you'd imagine they'll appreciate the "heads up" and will try to make some adjustments. Therefore you should also set up a follow-up discussion with the person. Ask how he or she is doing and show your true desire to help.

If you have one of the few who has repeatedly tried to correct an issue and is not making progress, or who really don't give a darn or even think you are wrong, then you may be stuck. If this is the case, I would request help. Usually best thing to do is to contact your human resources department.

By all means, I want you to get the best attitude, an empathic, informative and positive attitude before going into this conversation. Positive? How could it possibly be positive? Simply, because you owe it! You owe this conversation yourself, because you are an excellent leader who has to handle much more challenging situations like this. You owe it to your clients, who want to leave your company, your store, your location with the best possible experience ever. You owe it to your other team members, who expect you to handle challenges like this. And last but not least, you owe it to

🐦 **Jason Houck**
@MJasonHouck
"Show your personality. Be genuine in doing so. If you care about people they will care about you."
#TheImageOfLeadership

the person affected. Not only is the issue probably affecting the business of your company, it's also affecting the employee's career. Furthermore, it's important for the person that you address the topic and give him or her to resolve any issues before other team members do it in a non-tactful way. If this happens it can easily escalate and become a bullying issue.

Always remember, you owe it to Jane (or Jim).

🐦 **Sylvie di Giusto @Sylvie_diGiusto**
"Your most important job in your leadership role is to create more leaders."
#TheImageOfLeadership

Do a Dress Code and Grooming Policy Always Help?

To everyone who answers "yes," you are wrong. To everyone who answers "no," you are also wrong. To everyone who answers "it depends"—congratulations!

A written policy that includes rules and regulations in terms of dressing and expectations in terms of personal grooming is the best first step for any organization. Some companies even go a step further by including their requirements in terms of attitude and behavior, or usage of social media during and after work hours. From the perspective of a company and their leaders, the good news is that you can cover quite a lot of topics in those policies, and basically they are always written to keep in mind safety, hygiene, and corporate image. Policies need to be comprehensive; whatever is left unsaid will surely be worn or done at work.

The scope of a policy ranges from wardrobe pieces that are allowed or not, to daily personal hygiene maintenance that is expected, to even restrictions based on employees' weight or weight gain. The Borgata Hotel Casino & Spa in Atlantic City, for example, became notorious for their policy that stated they would fire any employee who gained more than seven percent of their body weight. The only exception was weight gain related to pregnancy. Employees who had been pregnant though only had ninety days after delivering their baby to get back to their pre-pregnancy weight. Does that sound fair to you? Or just terribly awful? Or like leadership heaven, because you obviously can dictate everything?

From any given perspective (the organization itself, their leaders and their employees), dress code and grooming policies can be helpful instruments, but at the same time they also can develop new challenges. Most leaders agree that the interpretation and acknowledgement of the rules that are written down in a dress code policy is one of the biggest ones and will vary from employee to employee. Like any other written statement made by management, some employees will read and understand it clearly, some are able to read in between the lines, some read them and give their best shot, and some just don't give a damn.

Another big challenge—and this is tremendously important for companies in a country like the United States, which has one of the biggest, greatest, and most wonderfully diverse populations in the world—is that such policies tend to be too vague and lack acknowledgement of cultural, religious or ethnic differences. Expats or immigrants may feel confused and offended. What we find important in the US may not be important somewhere else and to them.

For example, Americans tend to use less fragrance in the workplace and companies often limit the use of perfumes or cologne in their grooming policies, to Arabians, French, Spanish, or Italian people, fragrance is very important and major part of their daily grooming routine. Female employees from different cultures and religions may not want to wear makeup because it makes them feel like a sex object. While many US employees see the dress of their European counterparts as boring and standardized—not to say matchy-matchy— those same Europeans experience the American dress code level as very wide, broad, and forgive me—even sloppy. While in many European countries women enjoy a broader range of fashion at the workplace, many US employees view the same styles as too sexy. It's not unusual for many Europeans to wear the same outfit two or three days in a row, while others think it's simply unsanitary. And in countries where people don't have a certain income or the wherewithal to just drop off their clothes at the local dry cleaner (or even more conveniently, with the doorman), one's interpretation of wardrobe cleanliness might vary.

While we might think that unless someone works in a very creative industry such as fashion, entertainment or music, tattoos trigger a negative professional impression, tattoos and piercings are seen as "body art" in other countries, and exactly because it is perceived in many cultures as "art," it's nothing you would ever cover. There have been several legal cases where employees have argued that in their religious beliefs it constitutes a sin to cover tattoos of religious inscriptions.

While head covers might not have a place in corporate America, many religions such as Islam or Judaism require to wear them at all times. If your policy prohibits clothing that has a religious basis (Sikh turban, Jewish yarmulke, Muslim headscarf), you have to prove that such head covers pose an undue hardship on your company's business; otherwise you may face a discrimination problem. Even Sikh beards and uncut hair or dreadlocks can be cases for religiously driven exceptions. And policies that ban "Afro" hairstyles can trigger race-based discrimination lawsuits. Requiring an employee to shave his beard could be seen as discrimination if the person has a skin disorder that make it painful to shave. Some religions observe holidays that prohibit to bath or shower for a certain amount of time, which naturally might create an increase in body odor. And while body odor is something that most Americans try to avoid at any price, in some cultures a little body odor is considered to be natural, and doesn't offend anybody. In today's culture companies often want their employees to live healthy, and it has become popular that they even provide staff with opportunities to engage in physical exercise during work hours. What if body odor became an issue in such a case?

Companies with several locations in the US or even worldwide often forget that the requirements might be different from location to location. Alaska is not the first place I would link to a body odor challenge, while Florida might have to handle this issue very often—just all because of the difference in climate. I've done training for companies who have very strict policies in terms of grooming, since their employees handle beverages and food. More than once I've discovered that they have provided their employees with uniforms made of polyester. If we had to wear it eight hours a day at work, being dressed in polyester would make each and everyone of us sweat, even in Alaska.

Female employees often believe that dress code policies have more restrictions on women than on men. My personal theory is that it's based on the fact that women just have many more "irons in the fire." We have to deal with more hairstyles, coloring options, make-up, nail polish, pantyhose, shoe types, and visible body parts, while men basically have to maintain neatly trimmed hair and nails. (Although in terms of personal grooming, men have plenty of irons in the fire too, considering the fact that hair that grows in ears and noses, and socks and neckties can be pretty wacky). Nevertheless, women generally tend to think they are burdened with more regulations than their male co-workers.

Another observation I sometimes make is that people who are responsible for those policies in companies also us them to dictate regulations based on personal preferences and not by actual business needs. By all means try to avoid this, both in written policies and in the conversations you might have as a leader. If there is no detectable and measurable reason to cover tattoos, for example, don't restrict them, no matter whether you find them appropriate or not.

The best policy control often happens by the staff members themselves. Existing employees also tend to control if everybody follows the policies. However, they tend to keep a close eye on those who lead them. They'd rather forgive their colleagues instead of their leader, who might not be perfect either, or hasn't followed a rule or dealt with his or her own personal challenges.

If your company has implemented a dress code and grooming policy, your experts are probably aware of all these challenges. However, I want you to be aware of them too. Because during every conversation you have with your employees about these topics, please remember to avoid anything that could be considered discriminatory in terms of your employees' age, religion, race, national origin, disability, gender, or any other category that is protected by law. Before you talk to your employees about those topics, I always want you to consult with your human resources department.

Also keep in mind that very rigid dressing and grooming policies may eliminate certain potential employees from considering working for your company, even though they may be qualified and the best match for the position you are offering.

🐦 **Sylvie di Giusto @Sylvie_diGiusto**
"Dress code policies need to be comprehensive; whatever is left unsaid will surely be worn or done at work." #TheImageOfLeadership

Chapter 10
Moving Forward

🐦 **Patrick Allmond**
@patrickallmond
"A mediocre product packaged
well will succeed over a great
product with poor packaging."
#TheImageOfLeadership

I f you're looking for a great ROI, nothing is going to beat investing in your professional imprint. Especially nowadays when so many people are struggling to find a job, let alone find opportunities for advancement, the returns of investing in yourself can be amazing.

After reading this book do you consider to hire an image consultant? You may accuse me of being a bit biased (maybe a little), but the truth is that you want to set yourself apart from all the other people at work in a positive way. Especially in today's highly competitive business environment, you have plenty of other information to worry about. Let someone else worry about the details of your professional image while you focus on the trajectory of your professional career.

Over the years I've learned it's better to craft the way others are going to perceive you, rather than to sit back and hope it's going to be in a great way. In my corporate trainings I let participants write on a Post-it one word—just one word—they want to be known for. Afterwards they have to do the same for other participants of the seminar. They have to write down what comes instantly to their mind when they think about or see the other person. These Post-its land attached on their backs. I let them carry around the burden and weight of their public perception through the entire seminar. They don't know if the way they want to be perceived (on their own Post-it) has anything to do with the way other's actually perceive them. And most often it doesn't. There are those who are positively surprised by the end of the seminar when we disclose the secret, and those who aren't. And there are those who don't find any Post-Its on their back, quite a painful realization either.

I encourage them—and you—make today the day you take control of your image, of the imprint you leave in others mind.

I would like to close the book with a story I usually use to open my corporate trainings. I take participants on an imaginary shopping tour. They have to imagine themselves walking with me through a supermarket, and while I walk them through I talk about the importance of packaging design, the importance of positioning certain brands (or non-brands) in certain spots on supermarket shelves, and on the few seconds that are relevant for our decision to put a product into the shopping cart. If a product is a trusted and well-known brand, people usually will toss it in the shopping cart without a thought. But if it's brand new and unknown, packaging experts invest lots of time, energy and effort in order to make sure potential customers notice the product and to receive a positive first impression.

People sometimes consider the products we use and their packaging to be two separate things—the product is the thing we want, and its packaging is just a piece of trash to be thrown away. But the most successful packaging designs, however, prove that a well-designed package can complement or even enhance the product it was designed to carry.

It's the shape and size of the packaging, the colors and the images that influence a customer to buy, or not. Successful packaging designer sell an experience through their packaging. Perception, perception, perception; It's all about perception!

Usually I stop with my participants during this imaginary shopping tour in front of the shelf filled with salty snacks, and pull out a package of potato chips from my handbag.

Chips packaging is always fascinating. Because, the most successful brands have something in common. Usually the package shows a picture of chips. "What you see on the outside is exactly what you get on the inside" is the first message I want you to get from this. Not one word, even not a lot of talking and describing the chips can do as much on the package as the picture does. It shows what you get. Period.

The other lesson is that too often what's shown on the outside is not really what you get on the inside. Usually you don't find chips packaging with a see-through part or transparent packaging. Instead, the outside package shows perfectly shaped and intact chips in a fresh and appealing way. We all know the inside is somehow different. Yes, there are chips inside, but not those we saw on the outside. Inside, they seem more ordinary, and there are usually many that are broken into little fragments. But we still like them. We are still into them. We basically accept the scam. What's the lesson here? With a perfect appearance on the outside, people willingly buy into you and might still accept you if you're not as perfect on the inside. The other way around is invariably much harder.

Last but not least, there are expectations. I ask participants how this package of chips would look if we bought the spicy version. Specifically, what color would the package designer use? All of them say "red." What does the organic version look like? And most of them say "green" or "brown." Obviously we have certain expectations for what things look like; it's a pattern, a map—something our brain is already trained for, based on our experiences and personal history. Did you ever see a pink package of chips? A purple one? Probably not. And those expectations are the same for leaders. While leaders come in different shapes and sizes, there are still certain expectations of how we want them to look.

For participants of my training sessions, for individual clients I coach, and for the readers of this book, what I hope for is that they are aware of the importance of their packaging, that they have the ability to present a package that represents their product in the best possible way, that their packaging carries them even through tough times and upcoming leadership challenges, that their packaging doesn't distract anyone from the great things they are able to do, that their packaging stands out for the right reasons.

I hope this book is part of this advancement. And if you ever need help, I want you to reach out to me, because...

People Packaging
Is What I Do...

Index

Contributors

Amongst other things within this book you have learned how important it is to surround yourself with great people. It's me who is lucky to be surrounded by nothing but great ones:

Jeffrey W. Hayzlett	Foreword	www.hayzlett.com
Alvin Valley	Book Review	www.alvinvalley.com
Jay Townsend	Book Review	www.jaytownsend.com
Shauna MacKenzie	Book Review	www.bestkeptself.com
Carole L. Jurkiewicz, Ph.D.	Book Review	www.hofstra.edu

During a 5-day Twitter marathon I've asked my followers and friends to contribute their point of view to this book. This has been an incredible experience to say the least. People from around the world shared their opinion within a short and sweet tweet. From successful leadership experts, authors and speakers, to fellow image consultants or well-known fashion designers, to total strangers. Thank you very much to each and everyone who joined the conversation!

Fatima Sheikh	Chapter 1, 2	@FSCharlie
Brad Kellum	Chapter 1	@bradkellum
Gina Carr	Chapter 1	@GinaCarr
Agents in Style	Chapter 1	@RhodaWheeler

Carole L. Jurkiewicz, Ph.D.	Book Review	www.hofstra.edu
Heidi Deblaere	Chapter 2, 7	@hdeblaere
Andrea Hill	Chapter 2	@andreahill
Mark La Penna	Chapter 2	@MarkLaPenna
Cassandra B. Jackson	Chapter 2	@DCCooky
Sarah Hathorn	Chapter 2	@sarahhathorn
Jessica Kupferman	Chapter 2, 4	@JessKupferman
Dawn Gallagher	Chapter 3, 6	@YourHomeSpa
Nikk Smit	Chapter 3	@NikkBishopSmit
Mallory Sills	Chapter 3	@MallorySills
Megan Brandle	Chapter 3	@MegsImageGuide
Brandy Hartman	Chapter 3	@BrandyLotusgirl
Ranbir Puar	Chapter 3	@ranbirpuar
Beth Bores	Chapter 3	@bethbores
Laura Algueró	Chapter 3	@mypershopper
Joel Thomas	Chapter 3, 6	@joelericthomas
Meredeth McMahon	Chapter 3, 4	@MeredethMcMahon
Al Getler	Chapter 3	@AlGetler
Shanna Wu Pecoraro	Chapter 3	@SPImage
Marc Jacobs	Chapter 4	@marcjacobs
Maria Schwarz Esq.	Chapter 4	@Divorcemuse
Dean Deguara	Chapter 4	@Deandeguara

The Image of Leadership by Sylvie di Giusto

Cesar Pinzon	Chapter 4, 9	@CesarPinz
Jeff Belle	Chapter 5	@jeff_belle
Jo Saunders	Chapter 5	@JoAtWildfire
John Michael Morgan	Chapter 5	@johnmorgan
Summer Silvery	Chapter 6, 3	@_sumerae
Jeff Sherman	Chapter 6	@shermanspeaks
3DConsultsExecutiveD	Chapter 6	@3DConsultsExecD
Sarah D'Alexander	Chapter 6, 9	@dalexands
Susan Pierce Jacobsen	Chapter 6	@AmFamSusan
Kathy Kiely	Chapter 6	@MadamePrez
Jacqueline Peros	Chapter 6	@jmpbranding
Vaibhav Pandya	Chapter 6	@pandyavaibh
Carol Davidson	Chapter 6	@CarolDavidson
Bruce Van Horn	Chapter 7	@BruceVH
Kristie Kennedy	Chapter 7	@kristieykennedy
Maureen Klecha	Chapter 7	@MaureenKlecha
Bryan Bumgardner	Chapter 7	@BryanBumgardner
Emily Thomas	Chapter 7	@emitoms
Gordana Biernat	Chapter 7	@Powertalk
Pilar L. Davis Media	Chapter 8	@pilardavismedia
Nic	Chapter 8	@stylebrute
Mark Sanborn	Chapter 9	@Mark_Sanborn

Faith Rim	Chapter 9	@FaithTheModGirl
Milena Joy	Chapter 9	@milenajoy
Phil Graham	Chapter 9	@philgrahambiz
Michael Shuttleswoth	Chapter 9	@Manstoolbox
Daniel Wallen	Chapter 9	@TheWallenWay
Jason Houck	Chapter 9	@MJasonHouck
Well Suited	Chapter 9	@priginasuit
Patrick Allmond	Chapter 10, 7	@patrickallmond

Disclaimer: Contributors are listed in the order of appearance. The views expressed within these tweets (or outside of this book) do not necessarily represent those of Sylvie di Giusto. Sylvie does not guarantee the copyright on the quotes provided, or she did not chose those quotes because she endorses the products or services these followers offer.

Acknowledgements

This book is a result of my journey through two career paths: one in the field of human resources, the other one as a professional image consultant. During the first path I was happy to meet someone who is not just a great leader, but who also left me with a lasting impression. Until today I think about the valuable time I was able to work with and for Dr. Matthias Bellmann. I still consider the advice he gave me, I quote him, and I refer to him… long after our interaction has ended. His attitude, approach, and style has become a touchstone for myself.

This book is also written in memory of the great Michele Savoia, whose path I was lucky to cross during my second career path at the Fashion Institute in New York. We had many plans, one of them was writing a book. Unfortunately faith had other plans with you, Michele. But, I know you are pleased to see it finally happened. I'm sure that god has never been dressed better since you have joined him.

The moment I experienced Jeffrey Hayzlett walking on a stage I knew there is no better person and leader to write the foreword for this book. He represents everything I want my readers to take away: authenticity, confidence, respect and self-control. Thank you very much for being a role model and for encouraging me to "-----" in the tall grass.

Thank you to the great people who supported me by providing their personal point of view to this book: Alvin Valley, for being much more than a king of pants by encouraging women to always have an unconditional belief in themselves. Jay Townsend, a giving heart and soul from the first moment I've met him and one of the many reasons to join the National Speakers Association. Shauna MacKenzie, my first "internet blind date" ever, who is such an incredible industry pioneer and instead of being a competitor she became a great friend. And Carole L. Jurkiewicz for the great opportunity to serve you and your students.

I want to thank all my customers for trusting me to be their source and partner for their personal, professional or corporate image. I'm grateful for the pleasure of working with each of you – individuals, corporations, or students. Customers like you make my job easy and enjoyable.

I also want to thank the many leaders who I've seen, observed, met, worked with, and studied throughout my career, and who have become examples in this book. To those in the category of the great ones, I'm grateful that you exist. To the not so great ones – you may still not realize that you need help, but I do appreciate the stories you provide of what-not-to-do.

Thank you to Thomas Hauck, my editor, for helping me make sense of the clutter of thoughts flying around within my head, and for giving me the much needed direction from time to time, not only about writing.

Big brothers are born first to lead and protect the little ones that come after them. So is mine. Only the luckiest girls have a brother like I do, who is also my living proof that you have to hold on tight to your dreams.

Last but not least, but always first and most important in my heart, thank you to my two wonderful children and to my husband, for their endless love, their support and their patience – especially with the workaholic in me. Words can simply not describe how much I love you.

Mobile App

Haven't you downloaded the app, yet? Go to theimageofleadership.com to download the mobile app "The Image of Leadership". With the FREE app you can:

- get a daily dose of professional image tips and tricks.
- take a look at Sylvie's bookshelf and see what's on her reading list.
- navigate easily through New York by using Sylvie's map of favorite places.
- meet and greet all contributors to this book.
- hire Sylvie as your coach or for your corporate event.
- receive a special offer if you book your consultation via app.
- follow Sylvie on Twitter.
- sign up for Sylvie's monthly newsletter.
- do so much more …

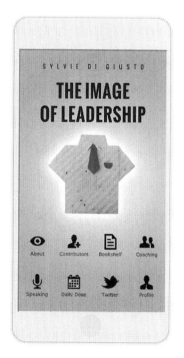

Go mobile now!
www.theimageofleadership.com

Please, also connect with Sylvie on any social media outlet.

Twitter: @Sylvie_diGiusto
LinkedIn: www.linkedin.com/in/sylviedigiusto
Google+: www.plus.google.com/+SylviediGiusto
Facebook: www.facebook.com/ExecutiveImageConsulting

Or, simply send her an e-mail: read-me@theimageofleadership.com

Please, leave a review on Amazon

Thank you very much for reading "The Image of Leadership". If you enjoyed this book or found it useful I'd be very grateful if you'd post a short review on Amazon. Your support really does make a difference and I read all the reviews personally so I can get your feedback and make this book even better.

Thanks again for your support.

Sylvie di Giusto
People Packaging is what I do ...

36485991R00109

Made in the USA
Lexington, KY
22 October 2014